HYDROPONIC GARDEN SECRETS

A proven system for beginners to grow vegetables, fruits and herbs without soil faster with a simple 8 step formula

OLIVER GREEN

Table of Contents

Introduction

G ardening is one of the most common interests of people around the world. Everyone wishes to produce his or her own little corner of garden production. A garden can also be the source of relaxation for an individual, as well as for personal satisfaction.

Hydroponics has been the dream of gardeners for over a decade. In the 1920's, in Munich, an experimenter and horticulturist named Heinrich Dorner discovered that by placing plants in a controlled environment with their roots in water, they would grow faster and with better results than traditional gardening methods.

During World War II, this theory was tested at the University of California at Berkeley. The results were amazing; it was found that with hydroponics, a plant could be grown in the casing that only contained 10% water and everything else could be cut to reduce weight. This led to new techniques for water conservation and new methods of selecting plants for landscaping purposes.

In the 1950's, hydroponics became popularized by Dr. Luther Burbank, a horticulturist who attempted to create an entirely new breed of the plant by using new hybridization methods. During the 1960's, many more seeds were sent off to space using NASA's space program. Pots were sent up as part of the program for test runs but apparently, all perished after returning to Earth due to the different conditions they faced. However, it is rumored that one survived and is now thriving in a secret location somewhere on Earth.

Hydroponics is growing plants without soil. It's a technique that uses the power of water to nourish the roots of your plants instead of dirt. Hydroponics produces high yields, with minimal effort and fewer pests than traditional growing methods. It helps to alleviate the need for pesticides, which have adverse effects on both humans and insects. Hydroponics is having a little revival, and for good reason. It offers a lot of advantages over traditional gardening methods. Hydroponics is also becoming increasingly popular, and people are taking advantage of the way it can help them grow their plants.

It's a proven technique used by experts for decades. It doesn't require soil, pesticides, or chemical fertilizers. Instead, it relies on the water flowing through your hydroponics system. Plant roots absorb up to three times more water than they exhale and all needed nutrients are absorbed, even during dry periods. To keep your hydroponics system running smoothly, we highly recommend using nutrient-rich water. The more nutrient-rich water that your plants get, the better it will turn out. The nutrient-rich water used in hydroponics is easily recycled and can be used for other purposes, making it a sustainable alternative method to traditional gardening.

Hydroponics is becoming more popular because it is inexpensive and allows you to grow fruits and vegetables that would otherwise be difficult or impossible to grow in your home garden. Hydroponics can also be used in an office or school environment and is not limited to just fruits and vegetables. With hydroponics, you can grow cannabis indoors with a minimal amount of human intervention. There's nothing to worry about pest infestations or diseases. You also won't have to be concerned about how much sunlight your plants receive.

Hydroponics allows you to grow a wide variety of vegetables. You can even grow fruit if the right equipment is used (such as hydroponic systems that produce "grow lights" for germinating seedlings). Hydroponics allows you to create nutrient-rich pools for different types of plants, which can then be planted together in your garden. In addition to vegetables, you can also grow strawberries, pumpkins, melons, and many other common fruits.

The most common form of hydroponic garden is actually called a closed-loop system. The closed-loop system uses recycled water and nutrient solutions to grow your plants in completely sterile conditions. This ensures that your plants will not be exposed to any pathogens from the ground or from pesticides used on the plants before harvest.

There are also more modern systems that do not use recycled water or chemicals to grow your plants but use only natural resources. These systems use nutrients and light to produce the plants you desire. If you prefer something a little more hands-off, you can even use some type of automated hydroponic system that relies on computer controls and sensors to monitor plant growth. Without the need for constant attention from you, these types of systems give you much more flexibility.

Chapter 1.

What Is Hydroponics?

light
substrate
overflow tube
water+nutrients
timer
water flow
water pump
air stone
air pump

History of Hydroponics

Our beginnings go back all the way to the 1600s. Hydroponics, or "water culture," is the oldest known form of plant cultivation. Since that time, hydroponic gardening has grown in popularity and range of application.

The original purpose of hydroponically growing plants was to supply fresh products for people who were unable to work in the fields due to a lack of irrigation or storage facilities. The invention of the hydroponic growing system made it possible for indoor growing on an industrial scale.

Since then, hydroponic gardening has expanded its applications to include environmentally-friendly gardening, as well as food production for animals and human consumption. As such, it has become a very useful tool in maintaining crop quality, increasing yield, and reducing food safety risks associated with traditional methods of agriculture.

Hydroponics is a great way for farmers to grow high-quality crops at minimal cost—there are no pesticides, no herbicides, no chemicals whatsoever. Instead, all you need are nutrient-rich water and trace elements—things like iron, magnesium, calcium, nitrates, and phosphates (salt water).

Hydroponics has become a worldwide phenomenon in the last 50 years, especially with the advancement of LED lighting. Due to the strict rules governing genetically modified organisms, hydroponic farmers have had no choice but to use non-GMO plant materials.

Gradually, new strains were created, and now farmers have access to a wide variety of organic seeds and plants. Hydroponic gardening changed the way plants are grown, and now seeds and plants are grown in completely natural environments, thanks to LED lighting.

Why is Hydroponics Interesting in Today's World?

Hydroponics is the answer to the growing concern for food production and food quality. Agricultural land worldwide is fast becoming short and that may lead to scarcity of food or insecurity of the food supply. Additionally, the productivity of farmlands is declining over time. Soil infertility is equivalent to low-quality food. The old system of rotation can only work for a certain number of years without depleting soil quality.

Through hydroponics, individuals may be assured that food is always available and that the crops are easy to harvest. Also, in areas with non-arable land, crops can be grown. Hydroponics ensures that to grow well, the plants or crops get the nutrients required.

The Growing Process of Hydroponics

The Era of Astonishment

In some parts of the world, we are still living the ordinary life, with all the necessary facilities and with the help of natural resources like in African and Asian continents. But at the same time, we are also the human species who are learning and working on the concept of artificial intelligence.

What Have We Done So Far?

In our short span of human life, we have attained all the necessary facilities of living with some magical technological and science inventions such as mobile phones for excellent communication, motor vehicles for a luxurious life, military weapons for hegemony establishment and who can forget the ongoing era of the digital world. Overall, it's a digital age and a period of technological advancement.

New Way of Plantation

Indeed, it's a new era because today we have changed all mathematics of nature by growing plants without soil. It is quite surprising and astonishing, but it's a fact now. Developing a plant without soil is known as hydroponics. So, now let's understand this term and method of plantation profoundly and figure out the growing process.

Hydroponic—What Does It Mean?

We know it's pretty confusing and astonishing enough when discussing farming and gardening without soil. Since our childhood, we have been watching the growing process of wheat and fruits through the land. And it seems like a pretty extraordinary thing. Science says, when we grow the plant roots with water and nutrient solution without soil, it is considered as a hydroponic process.

Hydroponic, the term looks like an arduous phenomenon of science and is hard to explain. But it is quite simple because the name of hydroponic says 'the growing of plants or farming without soil.' It means that with the help of nutrients and water we can grow any plant. So, let's understand this deeply.

We all have read about the growing process of plants in our school's science book. The method of making glucose from sunlight and the chemical found in plant's leaves and the overall process is called photosynthesis.

The Theory behind Hydroponics

The theory behind hydroponic says that through water, growing medium (reservoir), and nutrients we can build a plant more effectively rather than soil-based growth. In a nutshell, the sole focus behind this theory is that experts want to eradicate every possible obstacle or barrier between plant roots and water, nutrients, and anything necessary for healthy growth.

$6CO_2 + 6H_2O \rightarrow C_6H_{12}O_6 + 6O_2$ is the sole process of photosynthesis. It means how a plant grows and what kind of element and things they need in their growing stage.

The plant grows through a process called photosynthesis. In this particular process, they use a chemical that is present in their leaves called chlorophyll and sunlight to convert water and carbon dioxide, which is present in the air, to produce oxygen.

And if you have noticed that, then you can identify that the soil is not mentioned here to grow the plant. And this is one of the most significant scientific proofs about the growth process of plants without soil.

The Growing Process of Hydroponics

After discussing the chemical equations, methods, and theory behind the plant growth, now let's figure out the process of hydroponics. So, it is pretty much clear now that you need water, sunlight, and nutrients.

We use soil to obtain water and nutrients, and if we get them without ground, then there is no need for land for the plant growing process.

And that is the sole theory behind the concept of hydroponics. Hydronic means to build a plant in water and most of the people called it the growth of a plant without soil.

Why Grow Plants Hydroponically?

Hydroponic is one of the biggest questions that is roaming all around the minds of people about the hydroponic process because our generation is now used to it. From our primary education to higher education, we learn how a plant grows from the soil by doing the natural process of photosynthesis, and suddenly a new term comes and redefining all the essential learning of people.

Plant and nature experts say that there are numerous benefits of growing plants through the hydroponic process. While doing the experiment process and growth, some researchers have found some extra-beneficiary growth of the plant through the hydroponic method.

The Secret of Hydroponics Success

If you want to be successful in the hydroponic industry, then you only need skills, dedication, and must have a keen desire to grow crops. It is not necessary that the person who is going to do hydroponic gardening must have previous farming experience, but it can be very helpful in understanding things in a better way.

With limited resources and a surging population, traditional farming is on the back foot as there is a scarcity of land; that's why several growers are looking forward to hydroponic farming.

According to the latest report, it is stated that by 2050, there will be a drastic jump in the overall population that is from 7.3 to 9.8 billion. Due to this reason, there is a need for food that will surge from 58% to 98% in the coming 30 years.

Farmers are concerned with regards to this as land is not available for the crops to grow. Thanks to hydroponic farming that has allowed growing the plants. The recent trend of hydroponic agriculture has captured the minds of farmers up to a great extent; that's why they are shifting from traditional farming to the hydroponic system.

The main benefit of this farming is that it is very versatile; the system of hydroponic can be placed anywhere, etc.

CHAPTER 2.

The Advantages and Disadvantages of a Hydroponic System

Advantages of Hydroponic Gardening

Improved Genetic Health

Plants in a hydroponic system are not only provided with nutrition that has an almost perfect composition, but they are also safeguarded from many potential pests that they could otherwise come into contact with when growing in the soil. This allows the plants to reach a higher level of genetic health. As the saying goes, 'you are what you eat.'

High-scale Production

Although hydroponics can be used to create your variety of plants at home, an often-surprising fact is that the hydroponic process is responsible for providing food to millions. The science has now been enhanced to a level at which more fruit, vegetables, and herbs can be produced at a higher quality than ever before! Yields from growing hydroponically are at least 20% greater than with growing with soil.

Affordable

Hydroponics will allow you to say goodbye to the often-costly ordeals of obtaining prepared soils and plant protection products. On top of this, most of the standard gardening tools (e.g., trowels, shovels, forks) are not needed.

Less Time, More Produce

The process of planting becomes a breeze because you will no longer have to spend time preparing soil between plantings. On top of this, your plants will be able to mature faster, generating an abundance of beautiful products.

Vegetables, Fruits, and Flowers Grow Healthier

With hydroponics, plants get the right kinds of nutrients in the right amounts at the right time, which means that they contain the correct nutritional values in the product. Studies show that there is 50% more nutritive content in crops grown in hydroponic gardens in contrast to traditional ones.

Faster, Better Results Are Achieved

Since nutrients are introduced and adjusted in the water, the plants feed directly and do not expend much energy tracing and extracting the needed supply of nutrients. They grow faster, bigger, and in superior quality. In this sterile and controlled environment, you will get twice the yield from your crops.

Hydroponic Gardens are Easy to Maintain

You can have a garden without soil indoor or outdoor. You require less labor in the setup and upkeep of a hydroponic garden. You don't need to test your soil or setup a plot. You can also use commercially available pH-balanced nutrient solutions.

You Can Grow and Enjoy Your Crops

A lot of people worry about the chemical content in their food because of inorganic fertilizers, insecticides, and other plant sprays. Growing your vegetables and fruits at home can give you the peace of mind that what you are eating is fresh and free from chemicals.

In a hydroponic garden, it is easy to harvest vegetables, fruits, and flowers. Moreover, you save more money.

You Can Grow Plants Anywhere

You only need a growing medium, water system, nutrient solution, and a light source, and you're good to go. Remember that plants will grow if their needs are met.

You Save Space

Unlike in soil gardens, you cannot have plants grow too close together or they will fight each other for nutrients. In a hydroponic garden, you can place plants with small roots together, and they will grow just as big and healthy as a traditional garden.

You Help Protect the Environment

Traditional gardening leads to the degradation of soils as high amounts of potassium, phosphorus, and calcium are introduced to it through fertilizers. Hydroponics is a good way to reduce the amount of arable land.

Also, you need far less water for a hydroponic garden than you would in a soil-based one, which contributes to conserving our Earth's water.

Hydroponic Gardening is Fun and Relaxing

Hydroponic gardening is advantageous not only to commercial farmers but also to home gardeners and those who are looking for hobbies. Soil-less gardening is a fun, innovative, and a great way to relax or spend time with your family. Additionally, there is much less physical labor involved in hydroponic gardening as compared to conventional gardening. It is a great stress reliever, as well. What can be more relaxing and rewarding than seeing the fruits of your labor literally, right in your own home?

There is Little Chance of Environmental Degradation

Fertilizers are not required in hydroponic farming. Additionally, you don't need to worry about changing seasons and weather conditions. Often, bad weather leads to the destruction of prized plants, flowers, and crops that you've worked so hard to cultivate, but with a hydroponic system, you can avoid these natural disasters.

There is Very Little Wastage of Resources in Hydroponic Farming

Waste products are reduced because dirt and soil are not utilized. Water is easily disposed of in a clean and proper way. This reduces the possibility of over or under-watering. The supply of nutrient water is regulated; therefore, you will not have to double-check if the water is enough or not.

The money you invest in preparing a garden and maintaining it is returned through products that you can eat or sell for profit.

Safer and Less Need for the Use of Pesticides and Chemicals

With hydroponic gardening, you also eliminate the possibility of pest infestation, therefore also removing the use of pesticides. This leads to a much healthier garden and products.

Improved Home Environment

Hydroponic gardens are some of the most beautiful gardens to have in your home. You can drastically upgrade the look of your environment through hydroponic gardening. Just as the site of an aquarium in your house is breathtaking, so is the site of plants in your home.

The Relieved Strain on Your Budget

Food is expensive, even more so are fresh fruits and vegetables. You can make a great cut in your household budget by simply utilizing your free space by having a hydroponic garden.

Enriched Skills

A Hydroponic garden is not just a garden, but a botanical laboratory of its own kind. You get to learn a lot about plants—how to take care of them, their basic requirements, and how to maximize yields. You also learn how to utilize your farming skills as you get exercise and learn how to create a scenic, green landscape around your compound.

Chapter 3.

Disadvantages of Hydroponic Gardening

Cost of Setup

Many traditional hydroponic setups can be quite expensive when you buy growing tents, lighting systems, and more. Although, prices are coming down due to LED lighting systems and other advances in technology. There are affordable hydroponic systems available, though you are limited in what can be grown in these.

Space Requirements

Depending on the system you choose, it will need space indoors, perhaps in a garage or spare room. Some people will grow in their attic or basement, though if space is limited, look at the Ikea-style growing systems that can be used on a kitchen countertop.

Learning Curve

Growing in soil is relatively easy and, although there is a lot to learn, can be done without any expert knowledge. Hydroponic gardening does require some knowledge to choose the right type of lights, ensure they give out the right light spectrum at the right time, monitor the pH levels, and more.

Regular Checking

You must regularly check your hydroponic system, monitoring nutrient and pH levels. Initially, this may be quite difficult while you get used to it, but as you get used to hydroponic gardening, this will require less work. It can make vacations a little tricky, but most hydroponic systems will cope with being left alone for up to a week.

Water-based Microorganisms

However, through proper hygiene and care the chances of this is minimal, particularly as you monitor the system regularly and can spot problems before they become serious.

Limited Range of Plants

Not all plants are suitable for hydroponic systems to develop in, and depending on the method you are using, you may only be able to produce certain types of plants or only a single type of plant at a time.

Diseases Spread Rapidly

Because the plants are spaced closer together and can often be the same type, if any diseases should get into the system, then they can spread very quickly. If should a disease is introduced, you will need to sterilize your entire system and start again. However, diseases are rare in hydroponic systems when proper hygiene is practiced, and new plants enter quarantine before introduction.

CHAPTER 4.

Overview of the Different Systems and How to Build Your Own

Wick Systems

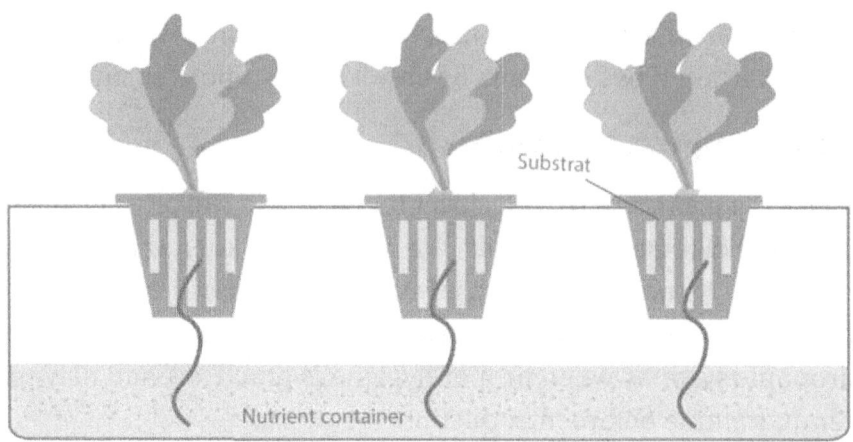

Substrat

Nutrient container

Wick systems are easy to understand and have simple components, cheap assembly, and low maintenance. Although they are part of hydroponic crops, they do not include water pumps or diffuser stones.

Since the plant controls the process, it will only absorb the liquid it needs. The wick must be long enough so that one end is submerged in the liquid mixture, and the second end is in contact with the plant's root system. An alternative crop substrate to the soil must be used. Sand, gravel, or pearlite are viable options since they can all absorb and retain moisture.

Standard hydroponic systems usually require expensive equipment and a deep understanding of cannabis cultivation. So why are wick systems so interesting? Although they still require conventional knowledge about the cultivation of marijuana, wick systems eliminate certain complications that could cause problems for novice growers.

The fact of not using land eliminates some risks such as pests, mold, and pollution. The wick provides a constant supply of nutrient-rich water. First-time growers tend to water the plants in excess, fearing they will not receive enough water. Wick systems, passively, provide plants with the right and necessary amount of water. Passive systems are quiet and do not require electricity. Even if complete kits are available, you can assemble a wick system using materials that are available at home. And, thanks to the absence of moving parts, the danger of falling or breaking objects is really minimal.

We have already commented on the concept and advantages of a wick system. Now, let's see how you can ride yours. A small observation before going into details: the most important aspect to consider is the quality of the wick. After all, it is an essential element of the wick system. The wick material will directly affect the speed and amount of liquid that is capable of absorbing and transporting the plants.

To make the wick, you can use every day homemade materials, such as nylon rope, the strands of a mop, strips of old clothes, or strips of propylene. Beforehand, you can test these materials by experimenting with colored water. When an hour has passed, you should be able to see how far and how fast the water has traveled. And finally, to get the best results, use two wicks per plant. Fill a bowl or small bucket with nutrient-rich water. Ideally, the container should be opaque and have a slightly smaller circumference than the growing pot.

Then, take the pot where you are going to plant and place both wicks in the center. A small hole should be in the base of the pot where the wicks can hang. Fill the pot with the chosen culture substrate and make sure the wicks are long enough to come into contact with the plant's root system and at the same time, be submerged in the fertilizer solution.

It is important to adjust the length of the wick. When you are satisfied, place the pot with the plant on the container of step 1, so that the pot is suspended over the water, with the wicks partially submerged in it.

You just assembled your first wick system! You will have to look at the level of the liquid mixture in the tank to know when you need to replenish it. The frequency between filling and filling will vary depending on the thirst of the plants.

Advantages

- The main advantage of the hydroponic wick system is that it is simple to build and easy to maintain.

- If you choose to keep it small or expand it, you can do it by recycling common household items and materials.

- Another important advantage is that it does not require electricity. This makes it possible to establish a hydroponic wick system in places that lack access to electricity, as well as make it more sustainable by not consuming electricity for artificial lighting.

- Speaking of sustainability, the hydroponic wick system is very efficient in the use of water. The system regulates itself since the supply of the water-based solution depends on the consumption of the solution by the plants themselves.

- In addition, hydroponic wick systems use less water and nutrients than other crop systems, due to the types of plants it supports.

Disadvantages

Throughout this article, we have mentioned the advantages of this system. But, despite its simplicity, it has certain drawbacks and limitations:

- Not suitable for larger and thirsty plants.

- The culture substrate can retain nutrients, causing the toxic accumulation.

- The water in the tank can remain stagnant.

- If the tank is sealed, providing oxygen to the roots can be a problem.

- The liquid mixture must be analyzed often to ensure an adequate pH.

To avoid some of these inconveniences, a water pump connected to an air stone can be added. It will oxygenate the water and prevent the accumulation of waterborne diseases. However, this increases the initial cost and requires that the wick system to be close to a source of electricity. By including the water pump, the system ceases to be passive.

Nutrient Film Technique

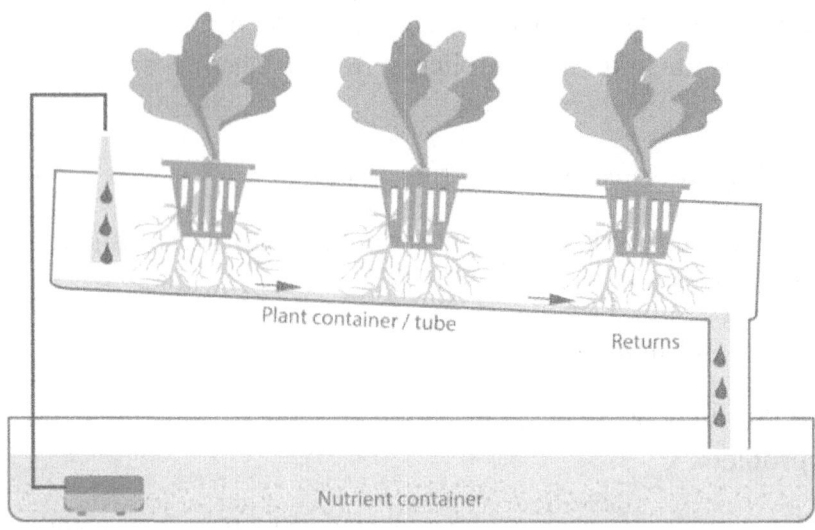

Plant container / tube

Returns

Nutrient container

Irrigation pump

An NFT system is a hydroponic system of hydroponic culture. NFT stands for nutrient film technique. The technique describes a hydroponic system that supplies the plants with water and nutrients via a thin nutrient film. In other words, a nutrient solution runs down a tube and flows around the roots of a plant.

The flow of water and nutrients ensures an optimal supply of the plant. Part of the roots is suspended in the air, allowing them to absorb oxygen. The lower root system is washed around and can absorb water and essential nutrients.

A water pump boots the nutrient solution from a water reservoir to the highest point of the NFT system. From there, the nutrient solution flows through the tubes and finally falls back into the water reservoir.

The Ebb and Flow System of Hydroponics

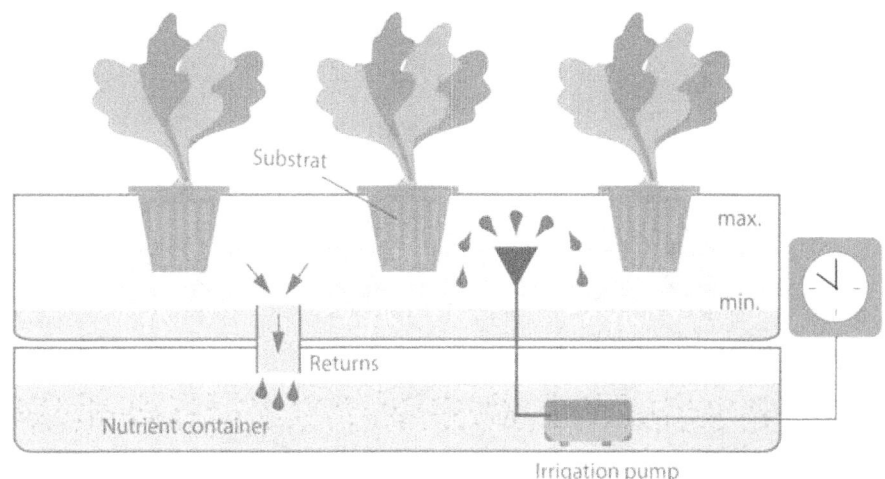

The ebb and flow system is an active and circulating system of hydroponics.

The system is active because a water pump boots the nutrient solution to the roots of the plant. In addition, it circulates because the nutrient solution flows back into the water reservoir after the flood, and the process then starts again.

Drip System

The drip system consists of a series of small pipes and droppers that connect your water tank to each of the plants in your garden. There is no limit. We could feed some plants or an industrial facility using a drip irrigation system. A timer then controls the amount of solution and the frequency of administration; neither one drop more nor one drop less is administered to the plants. You do not even have to be there to feed them.

This system still has its disadvantages. This will not be the easiest method to set up. Having a garden hose around your grow room will make things much easier for the average grower. Hoses should also be cleaned from time to time to prevent clogging. Algae and mineral buildup could stop the flow of water. This could result in one or more of your plants not getting the water solution they need. If your system distributes water under the soil, you will have no way of knowing if your plant is being nourished. You will notice a nutrient deficiency only a few days later.

Drip irrigation will also require monthly rinsing. This will help solve this problem. By regularly rinsing your system, you will clean the residue left by the slow flow of water. Finally, although this system requires less supervision, it requires more attention when you face it. You need to constantly check your plants for signs of poor health or disease. This is the only way to solve a problem in time. Particularly important for farmers living in extremely dry areas where water may be scarce. Drip irrigation will ensure you always have enough water for your plants.

Deepwater Culture

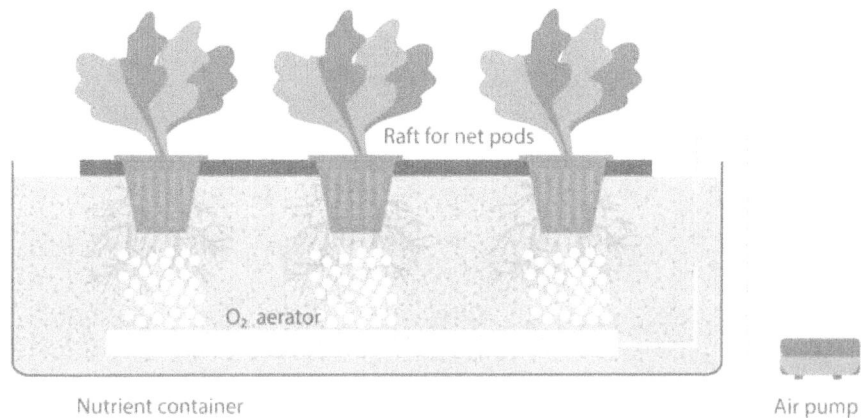

It is a special kind of hydroponics culture in which you grow in a ventilated nutrient solution. Here you will learn how and why more and more cannabis growers use DWC to achieve faster growth and higher yields.

While some cannabis growers simply grow their crops in the soil, other hemps use more elaborate cultivation techniques such as hydroponics. Deepwater Culture (DWC) is a hydroponic method of growing cannabis, which can have many benefits. Find out what makes a deepwater culture so rewarding and how you can set up your own DWC system!

Deepwater culture is a type of hydroponic culture that uses no medium. In a DWC system, the plants are hung in special pots or nets so that they stretch their roots down and immerse themselves in a basin of aerated, nutrient-rich water. Cultivating cannabis in a DWC system can bring many benefits compared to other farming methods.

The deepwater culture is an active hydroponic system in which the roots of the plant are suspended in a nutrient solution. Thus, the plant is always supplied with water and nutrients.

The plants are stuck in net pots and are fixed with a substrate. The mesh pots can be placed over the water surface in two ways: either you drill holes in the lid of the water reservoir, or you put the pigtails in a floating platform.

Aeroponic

Water nozzles/nebulizer

Nutrient container   Irrigation pump

This is one of the high-tech systems in hydroponic gardening. Like the NFT, the growing medium for the Aeroponic system is air. The plants' roots are misted with the nutrient solution every few minutes.

A timer triggers the misting pump, similar to the other hydroponic systems. The only difference is that there is a shorter cycle for the pump. It is a quite delicate and complicated system. There should be no interruption to misting cycles. Otherwise, the roots will dry out quickly.

CHAPTER 5.

Hydroponics vs. Aquaponics

Aquaponics

Aquaponic gardening is a food production method in which aquaculture and hydroponics are mixed. The method of raising aquatic animals such as fish, prawns, crayfish, or snails in tanks is aquaculture. The method of growing plants in a symbiotic system, in water, is hydroponics.

Over the last few decades, the supply of high-quality fish has been declining. The total number of fish available for American consumption has decreased through overfishing, habitat loss, and ecological damage. As a result, fish farms began to spring up as a way of handling the decline in the population of fish. Such fish farms have become specialists in aquaculture, rearing and cultivating aqua-life, mostly fish.

Fish farms quickly became the world's fastest-growing food industry. Aquaculture farming is very much like chicken and beef farming; there are large water systems and ponds full of water and fish. Fish farms are also used in pet stores and aquariums for bait, growing algae, and supplying fish and plants. It may also be used to increase a fish population that is endangered.

Fish farms, Mari culture, algaculture and advanced multi-trophic aquaculture are the various types of aquaculture; each of these systems produces different products and offers different uses. The culture of Mari is the cultivation of animals or plants that involve an atmosphere of saltwater. Many forms of shellfish, finfish, such as flounders, and sea plants, such as seaweed, are examples of these types of items. This type of system is developed either in the ocean, where the atmosphere is already suitable for the species, with large nets or tanks placed in the ocean water, or in tanks filled with salt water outside the ocean.

The most popular type of aquaculture is fish farms, and the purpose of this method is to produce fish for human consumption. Approximately half of the world's fish consumption comes from fish farms; in the last twenty years, this industry has tripled. Salmon, catfish, trout, cod, and tilapia are the most popular fish produced by fish farms. For the purposes of controlling the booming industry, many recent legislative acts have been produced.

Algaculture is the cultivation of algae, such as seaweed and phytoplankton. These product categories are intended for fish food, animal feed, dietary supplements, and human use. This particular type of system is very difficult to oversee, primarily the small algae, which is susceptible to small changes in the environment. Algae require a very specific lighting, temperature, and nutrition. There are two types of systems used to cultivate algae: open-pond systems and closed-pond systems. Open pong systems are primarily used because they are generally easy to construct, less expensive, and typically produce the most amount of product. However, controlling for light and temperature is difficult. Closed-pond systems are similar to open pond systems, but they are covered by controlling for both light and temperature. This type of system produces less product because it is usually smaller and more difficult to build. There are variations of different closed and open-pond systems, however, we won't cover this topic as in-depth as that.

Lastly, the integrated multitrophic aquaculture system is a more advanced system incorporating many different types of species into one system. The excrement from one species can be used as fertilizer for another species; for example, shellfish get their nutrients from shrimp and fish droppings. It is important to understand the basic components and how they work in aquaculture (or for our purposes in an aquaponic system) before starting a complex environment like this system. The purpose behind this system is balanced, you are creating a symbiotic relationship where both species benefit from each other's presence.

Hydroponics vs Aquaponics

They sound a lot alike, don't they? Hydroponics and Aquaponics? They are similar in one way, but vastly different where it counts. Hydroponics means, literally, grown in water. If you take the words aquaculture + hydroponics and put them together, you get aquaponics. Let's look at the two processes in more detail to see why one will be better for you than the other.

Ditch the soil. Both systems offer to grow a garden without soil. This represents a huge benefit. Soil becomes stagnant after years of cultivation, requiring a lot of fertilizer and/or rotation of crops. Simply replacing the soil during repetitive seasons of indoor growth becomes expensive, on top of that, the soil is easily contaminated with spores or pests laying eggs, perpetuating all of the diseases from one season to the next. Growing in the soil almost requires an outdoor garden, and living in a climate zone with harsh winters means you can only grow your veggies half of the year. Both systems offer value in growing without soil.

Instead of soil, you'll grow your plants in a biosystem of specially cultivated beneficial bacteria, and your very own circle of life will sustain both fish and plants. This healthy substitute for dirt is simple to produce, and you'll wonder why you never tried aquaponic gardening before.

Fertilize the water. Both systems require nutrient-based water for plant growth. Hydroponic gardening employs chemical nutrients, which represent constant overhead. You may obtain your growing medium from any number of suppliers, but let's face it: the uncertain role of chemicals in cancer and birth defects is generating headlines around the world. In aquaponics, you may grow organic vegetables through natural fertilizer produced by fish swimming around the tank. The advantage goes to aquaponics.

Design the right space. Both systems require light and a floor strong enough to withstand some pretty hefty weight. I was clueless. I imagined a sweet little aquarium with plants above it and was shocked to realize a twenty-gallon aquarium weighs a whopping 225 pounds. A concrete floor in the basement sounded smart, but I was hooked on the idea of cute goldfish and had a 14-ft. bay window in the dining room, so the scales became my enemy.

Figure about one inch of fish per gallon of water. If I have a fifty-gallon tank, you'll need fifty-one-inch goldfish. As they grow, that number decreases.

My research suggested that I needed at least a fifty-gallon tank, so I had to adjust my weight limits to six hundred pounds. If space and weight are an issue for you, hydroponics has the advantage in this case.

Both systems are going to affect your utility bills. The difference between them is that in hydroponics, the water may not be recycled. In aquaponics, the water must be recycled to formulate the rich growth medium to fertilize the plants. A high-water bill would make it cheaper to buy the product at the market, which makes aquaponics preferable.

Both require a growth medium that serves as an anchor for the plants, helps regulate temperature, and provides constant nourishment. In aquaponics, hydroton is a popular form made from clay. I wanted to get a product I was accustomed to using, but all of them were on the no-no list: sand, vermiculite, peat moss, wood chips, and pearlite. On the plus side, this represented a one-time purchase, and I could live with that. I see no strong value of one system over the other, because both require a mix to hold the plant.

Both systems require an investment in setting up the apparatus. A hydroponic garden is cheaper to start if you employ a wicking or water culture system. Both require a more complex design for some setups, and hydroponics equals the cost of aquaponics when you add a sump pump and additional piping. Aquaponics requires an investment in fish, but the cost will be less than continually buying chemical fertilizers for the water. In this case, the advantage goes to aquaponics.

However, the learning curve is definitely higher for aquaponic gardening. Because you are dealing with live organisms to create the fertilizer for your plants, it takes time and experimentation to get the right mix for ideal growth. If you require instant gratification, go with hydroponics. If you like a challenge, like to putter with details, and are willing to wait for results, go with aquaponics. For ease and learning the advantage goes to hydroponics.

To better asses these differences, you first have to have a clear idea of how regular gardens work.

Regular Gardening

- Plants are planted on the soil, which provides a growing medium as well as needed nutrients.

- Sunlight and rain provide other needs for photosynthesis.

- Needed nutrients and water may be supplemented by the use of fertilizers and irrigation.

Hydroponic Gardening

- Plants are placed in an inert medium.

- Water is constantly pumped through the root for hydration.

- Nutrients are introduced through specially made chemical mixes dissolved in the water.

This system is often considered more advantageous compared to regular gardening because of the level of control that can be had on the environment. There is also improved hydration and better control over the available nutrients for the plants.

The chemical mixes can be customized according to the needs of specific plants and their current stage in the growth cycle. This translates to yields that are more consistent and improve production.

Aquaponic Gardening

- It is the same with the hydroponic system with regards to the nutrition and hydration of plants. The use of chemical mixes may also be implemented to aid plant growth.

- Fish and bacteria work together to create much, if not all, of the nutrients needed by the plants.

Here, you can see that, although relying solely on fish and bacteria might not give you the exact amount of nutrients that you want, aquaponics is also much more economical.

CHAPTER 6.

Hydroponics vs Aeroponics

In hydroponic cultivation, plants are grown in the absence of land and with the use of water. In general, it is possible to say that with this technique, plants grow thanks to the action of water enriched with nutrients.

In the first period, the plants are started inside inert substrates, such as coconut fiber, perlite, expanded clay, or other materials useful for the realization of substrates, to then pass into hydroponic systems, which provide, in addition to correct water supply, thanks to the presence of ad hoc lamps, the temperature, humidity and the right ventilation of the environment.

Aeroponics is an alternative form of growing plants, vegetables, and fruits that do not require the use of land or water.

With this cultivation technique, plants live and grow brilliantly and healthy thanks to a nutrient solution's nebulization, based on water and substances useful for growth, which is delivered to the roots with a special spray.

This technique should not be confused with hydroponics, where the most crucial element is not air, as in this case, but water.

Once the aeroponic system is set up, the plants are suspended with the roots in the air inside a grow room (or cultivation chamber), where they will remain until the moment of collection.

The growth and plant health basis are undoubtedly the constant control of temperature, humidity, and lighting.

Pros and Cons of Hydroponics

We have already said several times that the advantages of using a hydroponic system certainly concern reduced maintenance, the possibility of cultivating at any time of the year, and the opportunity to control the cultivation environment's climate.

More generally, the great advantage of hydroponics is in complete control over nutrients and, therefore, on plants' growth. Furthermore, hydroponically grown plants perform better than plants grown in the soil. Many systems of this type recycle water and reduce waste.

These soil-free cultivation systems use only 10% of the amount of water needed for conventional crops and are fairly easy to build and assemble. Hydroponic gardens do not require the use of herbicides or pesticides, precisely because weeds do not grow there, they need little space and do not depend on the growing seasons, because they use lamplight, which can be installed anywhere.

However, hydroponic gardens have some cons; for example, if the temperature is too high or too low, the plants could die or otherwise suffer severe damage even for a single day.

Also, the purchase of hydroponic systems and accessories may require a significant expense, especially if you are not an expert.

Pros and Cons of Aeroponics

Among the advantages of aeroponics, there is the efficiency and cleanliness of the cultivation environment in the absolute first place.

With this technique, excellent and thriving crops are obtained in a short period. Another significant advantage is the slight risk of contracting bacterial diseases and infections. On the other hand, a disadvantage, especially if you are a beginner, lies in the relatively high cost, because it requires purchasing a series of equipment. It is also necessary to have a dedicated indoor room, where you can install the aeroponic system.

Hydroponics and Aeroponics: Similarities and Differences

The hydroponic and aeroponic systems have many points in common: aeroponics is, in reality, a particular type of hydroponic culture, which also uses the benefits of air. To simplify and summarize, we can say that aeroponics is an evolution of hydroponics, to get the most out of the potential of plants in terms of yield and speed.

The main difference between the two techniques is that hydroponic systems come in many forms: plants can be suspended in water full time, or a continuous or intermittent flow can feed them. In a hydroponic system, plants grow with water and without soil, with the help of inert substrates. The two systems have in common the supply of nutrients that are delivered directly from the source and supplied to the roots.

However, the plants in aeroponics are never placed in the water but sprayed at a distance thanks to a dispenser that hydrates and nourishes the roots several times an hour, thanks to an automated system that guarantees regularity and punctuality. One reason these two cultivation methods have so much in common is that aeroponics is, in reality, a type of hydroponics. The main difference is that hydroponic systems can be of various types: there are different types, and for this, you can choose the one that best suits your needs.

A disadvantage common to both hydroponic and aeroponic cultivation systems is that relying on automated systems that require, therefore, electricity, they could require the use of expensive generators to be used in case of power outages. However, once set up and started, hydroponic and aeroponic systems allow you to save significantly compared to traditional cultivation techniques.

According to current phenomena, it is possible that forms of hydroponic and aeroponic agriculture will increase in popularity over time and become commonplace in all of our homes. What is certain is that due to climate change and man's unregulated action, the quantity of soil available for cultivation will tend to decrease, and its quality will continue to deteriorate. Therefore, more and more people will try to produce healthy food in their homes (many have already started to grow vegetables, tomatoes, strawberries, etc.). Hydroponic and aeroponic gardens and orchards can provide the right answer to these growing needs.

CHAPTER 7.

Hydroponics vs Soil Gardening

Arguments have always abounded on which is better between soil gardening and hydroponic gardening. Some people are of the opinion that soil gardening beats hydroponic gardening, while some others argue that hydroponic gardening is definitely better than soil gardening.

So, which do we believe?

Soil Gardening

Soil gardening, as you know, is more affordable because the equipment needed is just simple tools and types of machinery, nothing ambiguous. Plus, typically, you do not need to adjust so much about the soil as it does this itself, using its environment as a gage. Since plants will naturally grow in the soil, it is only natural for the soil to be gentle on plants. Overall, soil gardening seems so much easier than hydroponics, what is not to love?

Well, those are only the good sides; would you be able to deal with the bad sides?

First off, it takes longer for plants to grow in the soil. You will also notice defects late because it takes longer for these defects to become visible. What this means is that the defects would have done so much damage before they are finally noticed, ultimately making the recovery of the plants difficult and longer. This could take its toll on your money and your time.

Then, at the beginning of your plant's growth in the soil, it will require all the attention and patience as it is still tender and quite vulnerable.

You also have to deal with preventing bugs from feasting on your plants. This is an almost impossible feat, and it's better to stick with hydroponics if you can't deal with the bugs.

Hydroponic Gardening

In hydroponic gardening, you have total control over the nutrient supply provided to your plants. This will help minimize problems that usually develop from an inadequate nutrient supply in the soil.

You also skip so much growing time and get to harvest really quick because the nutrients come directly to your plants and your plants do not expend so much time and energy in search of nutrients, as is the case in soil gardening. They, therefore, spend most of the time and energy on their growth, which ends up happening fast. As a matter of fact, a plant grown hydroponically under the same conditions as one grown in the soil can grow fifty percent faster.

Plus, since your plants grow faster when grown hydroponically, you get to identify defects on time and fix them right on time.

At this point, I bet you now see just how much more beneficial hydroponics gardening is, and this is just the introduction!

Is Hydroponic Gardening Even Healthy?

The nutrients supplied in a hydroponic system are not in any way different from the one in the soil; it is gotten from mineral salts. What is different in the nutrient supply is, as I mentioned, that the roots of plants grown in the soil have to go in search of nutrients; that is what makes their root systems so large. Plants grown hydroponically do not have to do this, because the nutrients go directly to the roots and in the right amount. This lets the plant spend less time growing root systems and more time growing leaves and stems. What you get as a result is strong and healthy plants.

Gradually, more commercial growers are starting to embrace hydroponic gardening over soil gardening, because it is amazing that you can control the supply of nutrients to your plants and conserve space. This ultimately boosts yield and profit.

Plants that are grown hydroponically are also not as susceptible to diseases and pests as plants grown on the soil, because of how vigorous they are. The plants possess anti-pest and anti-fungal buffers that keep them protected. This means less money spent on fertilizers, fungicides and pesticides, and more safe foods, as the consumption of chemical-ridden plants no longer becomes an issue. Plants that have been sprayed with fungicides and other chemicals have detrimental effects on the health and this practice is worth doing away with.

Worthy of note is how much better a hydroponic system is for the preservation of the environment. Since water circulates throughout the system, it does not get sucked into the ground or evaporate quickly. So far, hydroponics has done so much for modern-day agriculture and contributed to the supply of fresh plants that are free from blemish.

This is a summary that I am sure already convinced you to consider hydroponic gardening. But just in case you are not as certain yet, we will get into the details immediately.

Why You Should Pick Hydroponic Gardening Over Soil Gardening

1. You Produce Chemical-Free Plants

When the soil is taken out of the equation, this translates to less pests and diseases to deal with. Plants grown hydroponically are not as susceptible to diseases and pests because of the absence of soil and how healthy they are. Pests tend to gravitate towards weaker plants and there are hardly weak plants in the hydroponic system, making pest infestations almost impossible. This in turn means that there is little or no need for fungicides and pesticides. In the end, you get plants that are not laden with toxic and unhealthy chemicals.

2. Saves Space

Since plants grown hydroponically rarely have bulky roots because they do not have to go in search of nutrients, you can grow more plants in smaller spaces. These plants will thrive; they have everything they need provided in the nutrient solution that is ideally measured and supplied. Planting your crops closely together rewards you with space-saving.

3. Saves Water

So much water is saved in the hydroponic gardening system. In the traditional soil garden system, a large amount of water is expended in watering the plants, this is done so that a significant part of the water gets absorbed by the soil and sucked up by the roots of the plants. Unfortunately, this system isn't such a great one because water ends up getting wasted.

How?

First off, after a good amount of water is poured out into the soil, only a reasonable amount gets to the root of the plant. The rest of the water either goes further down in the soil or evaporates. Whereas, in the hydroponic garden system, a recirculating nutrient reservoir is employed. Plant roots only take up some of the water at a time, the rest of the water is preserved for later. This preserved water in the reservoir is covered to ensure no evaporation occurs and water cannot seep through the bottom.

With this system, the amount of water that has gone into watering a plant in one day could be used for several weeks in the hydroponic system. So much water-saving!

4. Location

Unlike in the soil gardening where you have to worry about location and external environment hospitability, the case is different in hydroponic gardening. As I mentioned before, everything in the hydroponic system is under your control, you are the boss. As a result, you would not have to worry a lot about the location (you can do it anywhere); first, because you do not even need so much space, and secondly, you can control the external environment of the plant. Since hydroponic systems do not require so much space and strategic locations, you can set up your hydroponic garden in urban areas that have little space without worrying. You can also grow your plants close to the market, thus, reducing transportation costs. Regarding control of the external environment of the plants, you are in charge of the nutrient supply and the light. There are artificial lights you can use when there is little or no access to sunlight for whatever reason. The seasons have no effect whatsoever on the hydroponically grown plants because you control the environment, not the seasons. This means you can grow a plant in a season when it is difficult to grow it, this brings you more profit.

5. Impressive Growth of Plants

In soil gardening, plants take so much time and energy developing root systems for searching for nutrients, water, and oxygen. As a result, they don't grow as fast because not as much time and energy are geared towards developing the leaves, stem, and most importantly the fruit.

On the other hand, plants grown hydroponically get to grow much faster because they have all of the nutrients, oxygen, and water right at their roots (I would say at their fingertips if they had fingers, but you get the point). Since they don't have to do so much searching for nutrients, oxygen, and water, they can spend all their time growing. This way, they're grown in short periods, which means you get to have more growth cycles for other plants in a given time. Plus, the plants also grow bigger. As a result, you get more yields.

For emphasis, studies confirm that hydroponically grown plants tend to grow up to fifty percent faster and bigger than soil grown plants.

6. **Control**

Even though this has been said a lot in passing while explaining other points, this is a point too. In the soil gardening system, it is difficult to control a number of things, like the amount of water the plants get, the amount of nutrients gotten by the plants, the nutrient composition of the soil, pests, diseases, pH, etc.

In the hydroponic system, all these factors are easily regulated so you do not have to beat your head. You call the shots over what nutrients and how much your plants get, how much water your plants get and how much is preserved, the pH of the oxygenated solution, the lighting and your plants are protected from pests and diseases.

7. **No Weeding/Digging**

This is good news for some. Unlike in the conventional gardening system with soils where you have to spend so much time on dirt, taking out weeds, building mounds and the likes, there is no such thing in hydroponics.

Since you are not dealing with soil, lots of soil issues give way, one of which is weeds. It is annoyingly time-consuming to spend years doing this. With hydroponics, this problem is solved.

8. **Cleanliness**

No soil means there would be no problems. With soil comes all the unpleasant stuff like parasites, weeds, pests, and dirt. In the hydroponic system, you will not have to deal with this mess.

You can garden without getting yourself dirty.

Hydroponics is obviously the cleaner choice!

9. Cost

At first, the initial cost of hydroponics can look like a huge disadvantage. However, as time goes on, the ground pretty much levels up.

What do I mean?

It is much cheaper to set up a soil garden than a hydroponic system. However, along the line, soil gardening starts to cost more. Money is spent on things like fertilizers, herbicides, pesticides, fungicides, and water.

Hydroponics, on the other hand, costs more to set up, but most of these costs get cancelled out as a result of how effective the system is regarding water, land, or space use, little or no need for fertilizers, pesticides, herbicides and fungicides, quicker harvests, more yields and ultimately, more profit.

CHAPTER 8.

Is Hydroponics Only for Indoors?

Humidity

In order to maintain conditions suitable for plant growth, it is necessary to provide a number of parameters, the first of which is humidity. In conditions of high humidity, the leaves of plants grow larger. Their maximum growth is observed at 60–80%. But it is better not to stick to the extreme numbers and set the humidity at 65–75%. Cuttings will need more moisture—up to 90%, and 60% is enough for seed germination. During the late flowering, it is best to use minimal humidity to avoid mold.

Humidity is a relative concept: there is much more water in hot air than in cold air. The used percentage humidity parameter is associated with water, which air is able to hold at a given temperature. This indicator is completely unrelated to the total water content in the air. At 10° degrees F and 100%, the relative humidity of water in the air will be half as much as at the same humidity, but at 20°C. This means that any increase in temperature in the room will lead to a decrease in humidity.

Accordingly, if the lighting turns off, and the temperature drops, the humidity increases. So, darkening the room for the dark period of the cycle, it is worth running the hood for a few minutes to remove excess moisture. Otherwise, it will settle on the leaves in the form of dew and can serve as an environment in which pathogens multiply. If the lighting is on, the humidity drops, so do not immediately start the hood to keep CO_2 produced at night.

If the humidity has dropped below 40%, and the air outside is too dry to raise the humidity, ventilation is indispensable: you will need a household humidifier. The air outside is usually cooler than the one in the room; therefore, once inside, it heats up and loses moisture. So even if the air outside is initially humid, it is not suitable for increasing humidity in the greenhouse.

In cold weather, it is better to cover the ventilation so that the air in the room warms up. Plants produce a lot of moisture, so it is even possible to use a dehumidifier. Plants prefer stability, so sharp changes in humidity are best avoided. If the leaves are bent up, this may be due to a rapid loss of moisture rather than an unbalanced diet, so do not rush to add corrective substances: it may be a matter of humidity.

Ventilation

Ventilation is needed, powerful and reliable, capable of updating all the air in the room in one minute. However, if the fan is too powerful, it will be difficult to ensure constant humidity. You can use an exhaust fan that can replace the air in the room in 4–6 minutes—this is enough, and the atmosphere will be stable in the room.

It is necessary to use different types of ventilation in parallel: an exhaust fan mounted on an outlet in the wall under the ceiling, it will blow air from the room; an outlet with an air intake located on the floor, in the opposite corner to the hood of the room, while the air intake must supply air from the basement or from the north wall of the house, it will not interfere with installing a protective net from dust and insects, if this does not interfere with the passage of air; circulation fans will make the air in the room homogeneous, exclude cold or hot abnormal zones, direct them better directly to the stems, which will allow air to be removed from under the crown, making the spread of diseases and insects more difficult.

The exhaust fan is calculated simply. The volume of the room in cubic meters is multiplied by 12 (updating every five minutes—12 times per hour). The resulting figure is an indicator of the corresponding fan. But there can be various barriers to the airflow. Thus, a carbon filter significantly reduces fan performance if air from the outside enters through the pipe; each of its elbows is an additional obstacle. Too small air intake will reduce fresh air. All these factors can be considered by taking a fan with a performance 25% higher than the calculated one.

Carbon Dioxide

The plant feeds on sunlight while consuming the carbon dioxide needed for photosynthesis, during which the carbohydrate necessary for the plant is formed and oxygen is released. This reaction is a source of energy for metabolism and, ultimately, for all life on Earth, since plants are food for all life forms, including humans.

But the plant also breathes, while oxygen is absorbed, which, when combined with a carbohydrate, releases carbon dioxide and energy. The plant breathes day and night, absorbing CO_2 for photosynthesis and releasing it when breathing. As a result, more oxygen is released than carbon dioxide, although oxygen is not released at night.

Gas exchange of the plant is carried out through the pores—stomata, which are located on the underside of the leaves. In dry, hot weather, stomata close and the plant slows down metabolism. But even when they are wide open, water vapor vaporized by the plant interferes with the absorption of CO_2. In the hydroponic cultivation method, the root zone has an unlimited water supply, the stomata do not close, and a good supply of carbon dioxide supports the plants in continuous growth mode.

When the first plants appeared millions of years ago, the atmosphere was much more saturated with carbon dioxide than now. Perhaps that is why the mechanism of its absorption is imperfect, and additional doses of CO_2 to plants are useful. Increased carbon dioxide helps plants withstand elevated temperatures. Permanent ventilation will ensure the flow of this gas and remove excess moisture.

Frost-Sensitive Period

Frost can kill a crop or cause serious damage. To some point, severe frosts will even reach the walls of a greenhouse, destroying plants inside. Even plants that are generally frost-tolerant can be severely damaged if the frost occurs at the wrong time of the year. Virtually all fruit or floral buds are susceptible to frosting.

If frost is likely to occur at a time near the opening of flowering buds, fruit development may be stopped even if the rest of the plant is not affected. Frost consumes some young seedlings. Tender, lush young growth is more frost-sensitive. You need to know when frosts are likely to occur at a particular site and select crops that do not have a high risk of frost damage for that site.

Day Length

Along with temperature, it is the most important factor for the formation of flower buds and for the development of fruit. For some plants, for you to achieve a good crop, the appropriate sequence of day length must take place. For other species, there must be a minimum or maximum duration of a day before flower buds develop. For example, for flowering to occur, African violets require at least 16 hours of daylight or artificial light.

Brightness

The quality of light is just as important for some plants as the duration of the light cycle. Where light intensities are too small, many vegetables and herbs do not achieve the same quality or yield amount. Other plants require lower light intensities and prefer shaded environments. A location obscured by tall trees or surrounding tall buildings will have lower light intensities than one facing off the afternoon sun. A valley site may have lower luminous intensities than one on a hill or flat plain.

The Optimal Temperature in Hydroponics

The temperature of the air is a very important external factor for the hydroponic plant cultivating place. This factor largely controls the speed of chemical reactions, enzymatic metabolism, and the development of plants (germination, a transformation of vegetative buds into reproductive buds).

The temperature that the farmer must maintain in his fields depends above all on the geographical origin of the cultivated plant. Indeed, these have special requirements in terms of temperature throughout their development: for germination, vegetative growth, and floral induction.

It should be noted that metabolism is the set of chemical transformations that take place in cells or living organisms. These reactions can be divided into two:

- **Catabolism:** The process of degradation of molecules followed by the release of energy.

- **Anabolism:** Brings together the synthesis reactions of macromolecules that demand energy consumption.

How to measure the temperature, what are the biological, chemical, physical processes depending on the temperature, and then manage this climatic factor for optimal development of the plants?

To know the temperature in his cultivating space, the horticulturist will use a thermometer. Originally, this instrument consists of a glass tube in which expends a quantity of mercury or colored alcohol. These instruments are simple and accurate enough for horticultural use. However, mercury thermometers can easily break down and spill the toxic metal into the cultivating place. With high temperatures, mercury vaporizes in the air and can be inhaled by people in the growing space.

The digital thermometers are less harmful to the environment and more convenient for the farmer. The measurement of the temperature is carried out by means of a junction diode in which circulates a constant electric field. The temperature variation of the cultivating place varies the dynamic resistance of the dipole. The temperature is displayed directly on a screen (LCD), and most of these instruments also indicate the minimum and maximum.

Some models have an external temperature sensor (probe) that allows you to know the temperature outside and inside the shelter. This is important for heating management: the greater the difference in temperature with the outside, the more it will be necessary to heat to reach the desired temperature (set temperature).

Where to Place the Hydroponic Installation?

The best place to place a hydroponic installation is an enclosed space. A basement or a greenhouse is well suited. Also, the hydroponic system can be placed in a small room without windows or in the courtyard of a private house.

The base for the installation of the structure must be strictly even and stable so that the water and the nutrient components present in it are distributed evenly. When installing the structure outdoors, pay attention to the control of liquid evaporation and ensure reliable protection of the hydroponic installation from the wind. Installing the system on the street as a whole is an extremely inconvenient option. In addition, you will have to constantly monitor that the hydroponic installation does not cool down and bring it into the room even with slight decreases in air temperature. In the case of assembling the system in the house, you will have to make more efforts to organize additional lighting.

Chapter 9.

Are Chemicals Used in Hydroponics?

Chemical Buffer

In the root, the respiration produced is carbon dioxide, which chemically reacts with the irrigation water to carbon dioxide (wherein an equilibrium).

In the circulating water of hydroponics, the equilibrium lies, depending on the pH, rather on the side of the free hydrogen carbonate ions (see carbonic acid pH indication water). Hydrogen carbonate ions formed to continue to react with water.

Free carbonic acid acts as a weak acid. The carbon dioxide in the circulating water lowers the pH value. In the soil, the carbonic acid reacts with limestones to calcium bicarbonate (also called bicarbonate). For details see Karst weathering.

A chemical buffer substance causes the pH to change much less when an acid (or a base) is added than would be the case in an unbuffered system. The amount of base or acid that can be trapped by a buffer without a significant change in pH is called buffer capacity that is in the soil exchange capacity.

In this specific case, a buffer substance (carbonate or a substance that also keeps metal ions as a chelate in solution) is added to the fertilizer solution. If the water contains too many protons (because it is too acidic), the buffer substance binds a proton and the reaction equilibrium is shifted to the carbonic acid, carbonic acid is formed. This breaks down into water and carbon dioxide (CO_2) and the CO_2

releases into the air (see also the carbon dioxide bicarbonate system). All fertilizer salts of a strong acid with a weak base or a strong base with a weak acid act as buffer substances, a salt of a strong base with a weak acid is used to buffer the carbonic acid.

There is also a pH increase in the microbial oxidation of ammonium to nitrate (therefore, hydroponic fertilizers should not contain any ammonium salt-based nitrogen fertilizers), they are illustrated like this:

$$NH_4^+ + 2O_2 <=> NO_3^- + 2H^+ + H_2O$$

Too high a pH-value of the circulation water can also emerge to systems such as hydroponics oxidative stress due to iron toxicity lead with various symptoms on leaves (yellowing).

In nutrient solution culture, the elongation growth of roots is inhibited at pH values below four and at too high pH values (with differences in different plant types). Nitrogen supply with NO_3^- leads to alkalization and with NH_4^+ to acidification of the rhizosphere. (See also effects of pH on plant growth and nutrient availability depending on soil pH.)

Inorganic Fertilizer

Each aqueous hydroponic fertilizer is a complete fertilizer in which all the nutrients mentioned are added artificially. That is why different formulas and approaches have been developed since the 1950s.

"Some plants grow optimally with a certain level of ion concentration ratio."

Name of the ion	Formula	Concentration in the solution [%]
Nitrate	NO 3 -	50 to 70
Hydrogen phosphate	H 2 PO 4 -	3 to 20
Sulphate	SO 4 2-	25 to 40
Potassium	K +	30 to 40
Calcium	Ca 2+	35 to 55
Magnesium	Mg 2+	15 to 30

The dosage information for liquid inorganic hydroponic fertilizers can be found on the packaging of all products.

In the case of multi-component fertilizers, the ratio of the core nutrients nitrogen (N), phosphorus (P) and potassium (K) in% of the commercially available reference base is usually given as the "NPK value," for example (13/13/21). This means that the fertilizer is 13% N, 13% P 2 O 5, and contains 21% K 2 O, see also NPK fertilizer.

Ion Exchange Granules

Ion exchange granules are solid special fertilizers (NPK full fertilizers) for long-term nutrient supply in a hydroponic system. These provide the plant with a single fertilization over several months. They consist of synthetic resin granules, which are loaded with salts (nitrates, phosphates, and potassium salts). They also contain the necessary micro-nutrients.

When normal tap water is added, the ion exchange granulate is activated. It then naturally absorbs salts contained in the tap water and releases nutrient salts loaded in the resin in exchange. The salts dissolve over a long period of time (depending on the nutrient intake of the plant), whereby the nutrient concentration remains in balance. This ensures a mild and long-lasting release of nutrients in a plant-compatible concentration.

The synthetic resin not only acts as a carrier for the nutrient salts. It functions as a buffer to keep the pH stable. It does not dissolve, but only leaves used resin granules behind.

Organic Fertilizer

Organic fertilizers are often used as a supplement to inorganic hydroponic fertilizers because inorganic fertilizers are more expensive. Organic fertilizers are mainly made from animal meals, ashes from plants or animal bones, dung from fattening animals, and industrial plant waste.

However, the exclusive use of organic fertilizer has some disadvantages, which are:

- As it is a natural product, the chemical compositions and concentrations of the nutrients vary widely. This is because; these depend on many factors, such as the food for the animal, etc.

- Organic fertilizer can be a source of various plant diseases.

- Organic fertilizer is often difficult to process due to the different consistency and size.

- Organic fertilizers give off strong smells.

- Organic fertilizers can contain ammonium compounds to reduce the ammonia (which is emitted into the air and is therefore no longer available as fertilizer nitrogen); the ammonium must be converted to nitrate in an aerobic process using microorganisms, as in aquaponics. The conversion is usually carried out in trickle filters (see plant treatment plants). Oxidation during the irrigation phase is not desirable because the aerobic process consumes oxygen, which is then missing for root respiration.

Nitrogen supply with NH_4^+ instead of NO_3^- leads to reduced root biomass. However, with barley, it has been shown that the plants have to use less (sugar) energy to absorb ammonium ions than to absorb nitrate ions.

- If solid organic fertilizer is used, prior processing is necessary (crushing, sterilizing, homogenizing, etc.).

Chapter 10.

Fruits: The Best Plants for Your System

Fruits often require plenty of heat and water. You will need a balanced nutrient solution, with plenty of lighting and a weight supporting system. One troubling concept of these plants is that many of the vine or become top-heavy due to the fruit. You will want supports or hanging baskets to prevent any damage to the plants. Fruits also like growing at 70 degrees Fahrenheit. For melons, you will want to start with seeds, and then put the young plants in your hydroponic system, within two weeks after they start sprouting. A fruitful and nutritious formula will work best for these fruits.

Fruit trees require a lot of oxygen and water runoff. You also want plants like pineapples to grow at a pH level of 5 to 5.5. It takes two years for a pineapple to start fruiting. You can also twist the top off a pineapple plant and let new roots grow to get a new plant.

Berries are like pineapple and other fruits. They want warm temperatures, as well as 5.5 pH. It does take a year or two for the plants to mature and start bearing fruit. Most berry plants will fruit one year, grow the next, and provide fruit again in the following year.

Strawberries

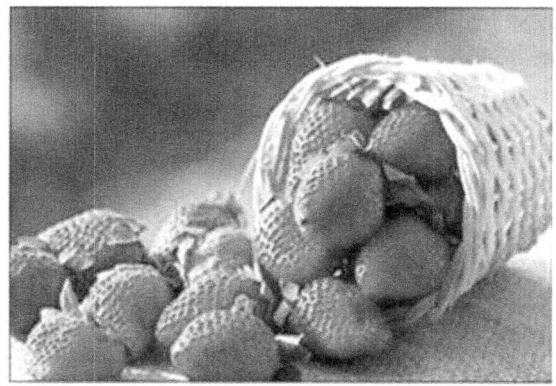

If you didn't already know, strawberries do very well in wet conditions. This means that they'd do well in a hydroponic system. Since strawberries do better in the hydroponic system than in the soil, the fruits will naturally be much larger, tastier, and fresher. These fruits are known to contain vitamin C and high levels of antioxidants, which are useful in protecting and safeguarding the body from free radicals, thus boosting the immunity of the body system. It also reduces high blood pressure and high cholesterol levels.

Strawberries are well adapted for growing hydroponic crops. These fruits are, in reality, one of the most common plants grown in commercial hydroponic production. For decades, the commercial farms have developed them in large-scale NFT schemes. Nonetheless, you will also enjoy tasty fresh strawberries by cultivating them at home and picking the fruits throughout the year to feed your entire family.

Blueberries

Blueberries will typically do better in hydroponic systems than in the soil. This is a result of their need for high acidic conditions, which is difficult to navigate through with the soil gardening system. Since the grower has control over the hydroponic system, he can set the pH and nutrient content so that it is perfect for blueberries. Blueberries are known to have one of the highest levels of vitamins and antioxidants, which are useful in the protection of the body, especially the nervous system and the brain.

In Hydroponics, you will develop blueberries well, a great fruit rich in vitamins for your meal. This plant needs longer to produce seed than strawberries, even up to the second year. Usually, they're built using an NFT process. Blueberries are challenging to grow from seeds, so transplants are suggested.

Tomatoes

Tomatoes are vining plants. As a result, they are great for indoor gardens because they do not need so much space to sprout and mature. This means you can grow as much as you want in small spaces. The hydroponic growing system makes it possible to keep an eye and control the nutrient supply to the tomato plants, so that you can keep growing tomato plants throughout the year, uninterrupted, with your set-up. Tomatoes are a plant rich in vitamin A, C, and folic acid. They contain potent antioxidants that help protect against the risk of heart disease, diabetes, and cancer.

Hydroponic hobbyists and commercial farmers have widely produced several forms of tomatoes, including regular and cherry ones. Botanically, the tomato is a plant, but most people find it as vegetables, whether they are dealers or customers. One point to keep in mind is that tomatoes need a lot of sun. And if you decide to grow indoors, be prepared to purchase any grow lights.

Cucumber

Cucumbers love water, so of course, it would flourish in a hydroponic system. Cucumbers can do well, as long as you shower them with needed care and give them a little space. They are rich in nutrients like folic acid, zinc, vitamin B, vitamin C, sodium, calcium, magnesium, and potassium. Cucumbers help regulate metabolism, lower cholesterol and slow down aging.

Cucumbers are a growing plant grown at home and in commercial greenhouses. Under the appropriate circumstance, they experience fast growth and hence offer very large yields. There are many styles and sizes of cucumbers, including thick-skinned American slicers, long thin-skinned European seedless, and smooth-skinned Lebanese cucumbers. In Hydroponics, everyone will rise well. Cucumber is a warm plant, so make sure to provide ample light and temperature to it.

Eggplant

Eggplants require conditions similar to tomatoes, except that they need higher temperatures. In low temperatures that last for a long time, they easily get hurt by the weather and do not grow well. It's also better to start planting them from a nursery and in spring (early).

Sage

Sage is usually used in seasonings for meat, cheese, and sausages. Altogether, sage takes about 14 weeks from seeding to sale. It takes about eight weeks to grow from a young sprout to a mature plug. However, it will need another month or a month and a few weeks before it becomes saleable. The plants can grow to about three feet wide and, therefore, require space.

In harvesting sage, do so before they bloom, then dry them in a dryer or in a room with a perfect ventilation on screens. Be sure during this period to protect them from direct sunlight. Next up, store them in containers that are airtight. You can then sell-off.

Peppers

Peppers can grow under somewhat similar conditions to tomatoes, but increasing nighttime temperatures and declining daytime temperatures increase the yield of fruit once plants reach their mature height. Not only do peppers bring taste and spice to your diet, but they are also small in calories and rich in vitamins and nutrients. Full of vitamins A and C and a decent source of protein, folic acid, and potassium give them valuable powers in the battle against infection and disease.

Peppers need the same rising hydroponic environment as tomatoes— warm weather and significant quantities of sun. Peppers sometimes take two to three months to mature. You may either start growing them from the nearest garden supplier's seeds or plants. Jalapeno, Habanero for spicy peppers are preferred varieties for hydroponic growing; Mazurka, Cubico, Nairobi, Fellini for soft peppers.

CHAPTER 11.

Vegetables: The Best Plants for Your System

Beans

Beans are easy to grow as they require little maintenance and are incredibly productive. Every kind of beans, from lima beans, pole beans, green beans, and even pinto beans. For pinto beans, you will need a trellis to support the plant. In about a week, your beans should begin to germinate and you can harvest in two months.

Spinach

Spinach is a very healthy and nutritious leafy green and grows well in hydroponic systems. It grows fast and is highly prolific. This means that you would be harvesting back-to-back if you are dedicated enough, and why wouldn't you?

The vegetable contains lots of essential nutrients, like vitamin A, vitamin C, zinc, iron, fiber, vitamin E, vitamin K, protein, magnesium, and copper. Its excellent antioxidant properties help keep the heart protected and reduces aging. Spinach also enhances proper digestion and reduces cholesterol levels.

Spring Onions

For commercial growers, this is another profitable plant to grow, as harvest can happen in just three weeks. Imagine how many harvests and how much yield you would get regularly! For spring onions, they are onions, but just young ones, harvested before they are fully mature. Plus, just one onion pot can yield dozens and dozens of onions!

Spring onions are healthy, containing vitamins A, B, C, and K. Its antioxidant properties protect cellular tissue and DNA from damage. It does this by fighting against the free radicals responsible for the damage. The nutrient content of spring onions also keeps the bones healthy and is used in the treatment of colds and flus.

Lettuce

Most growers grow lettuce because of how easy it is to cultivate; it does not need so much attention, so much space, and so much growth duration. In only a few weeks, you would've harvested them and with little effort. They contain vitamin A, vitamin C, iron, potassium, vitamin K, magnesium, calcium, and phytonutrients that boost metabolism, enhances body health, and protect the body from diseases.

Chives

Chives are best grown in a hydroponic system where the pH is controlled and set to suit its slightly acidic requirements. Chives need lots of light, at least twelve hours of light every day. It typically takes eight weeks to mature and then subsequently about a month to continue harvesting after re-growing.

Kale

Lots of people have continued to attest to how effective it is to grow Kale in a hydroponic system. It has been done for years by commercial growers. The vegetable is healthy and retains its delicious nature. Hence, it can be used for both home-cooked meals and restaurant dishes. Part of the reasons Kale will do better in a hydroponic system is its need for a slightly acidic environment, which is difficult for the soil gardener to achieve. As a result, Kale plants grown hydroponically tend to look healthier than those grown in the soil.

Peas

Peas, especially snow peas (also called Chinese peas), do not do well in high temperatures. They need to be planted in fall or spring when the weather is cooler. In high temperatures, well over 80 degrees Fahrenheit, the pods set poorly because of the plant's sensitivity to heat.

Before planting peas, you will have to decide which kind you'll be planting, as there are different types of peas; there's the Garden pea

(English), Snap Peas, and the Snow peas (Chinese). Each possesses different characteristics even though they are similar. For example, the Snap peas produce edible seeds and pods, so do the Snow peas. However, the Garden peas only produce edible seeds.

You can start to harvest the peas four weeks after it starts flowering.

Broccoli

Broccoli does well in hydroponic systems, but it will require sturdy stalking because it's a heavy plant. The plant is a part of the cabbage family and is mostly perennial. May is the ideal planting season for the vegetable, and by winter, it should be ready for harvest.

Cabbage

Cabbage, depending on the variety, often needs about two feet to grow out and spread. When starting out, start in Rockwool cubes until the plants are large enough to be transferred to hydroponic pots. You know they're ready to be transferred when they are able to stand. In the hydroponic pots, make sure that they're surrounded with the controlled medium. For a flush system, it's best to fill the tray under with water and then drain immediately, you don't want the seedlings to float out of the growing medium.

Cauliflower

The cauliflower is of the same family as the kale, cabbage, broccoli, and collards. Like broccoli, cauliflower require little maintenance; it can thrive in cooler temperatures and do not need so much attention and nutrients. Since cauliflower cannot be upright, you will have to come up with a way to prevent the body of the plant from getting soaked in the hydroponic solution. An idea is using a net over the solution, so that the roots of the cauliflower can grow through the net to get to the solution. You can also try using gravel to form a layer that roots can also go through, but the body stays above. Twice a day is sufficient to supply the plant with nutrients via drip irrigation so that the roots do not get soaked.

Watercress

Watercress is a perennial crop and a part of the mustard family. It grows best between mid-autumn and spring. Harvest the watercress before it flowers, else the leaves become inedible (except it's not being grown to be eaten). Generally, they're easy to cultivate and even easier with the hydroponic system.

Parsley

A hydroponic system is perfect for parsley. The plant has a lengthy tap root and so will require a hydroponic container that is at least twelve inches to accommodate its roots.

Potatoes

Potatoes are root crops; most of their growth will happen in their root, and they will need a hydroponic system with enough depth so that they can grow effectively. As root crops, this does not mean that all their growth is directed to the roots, the foliage and stems grow too.

Potatoes will also require enough space as it grows in the root area, otherwise, their growth may become stunted.

Swiss Chard

Swiss chards are beautiful and colorful plants that can be used for your salads. They will make your meal look even more colorful than the typical green colors.

Swiss chards do well in hydroponic systems and will gladly beautify your hydroponic garden with its lovely colors. Plus, they're good for the body, as they contain phytochemicals necessary for proper body health.

Radishes

Radishes are also great with other vegetables; they add a wonderful flavor to your plate.

You will have little to no issues planting them in your hydroponic garden because they happen to be an easy-to-grow vegetable, whether it's in a hydroponic garden or a soil garden.

They typically do better in cooler temperatures and with no lights. Within a week of planting the seeds, you should begin to see its seedlings, and it's always best to start from its seeds.

CHAPTER 12.

Herbs: the Best Plants for Your System

It does not matter whether you cultivate herbs for therapeutic or culinary purposes; a hydroponic system is a nice way of growing them. To do so, there are several reasons: the first reason is that herbs are growing more rapidly. To this, you can also add that the herbs arise with more flavor and scent than soil-produced equivalents do. Works also reveal that hydroponic herbs produce aromatic oils more than up to 40%.

Herbs are concerned with water, temperature, and light, like the other plants. Growing herbs with hydroponics, regardless of the climate or season, help you keep producing herbs. Hydroponic processing requires less energy and eliminates the use of water.

Although all herbs in a hydroponic system should not be hard to grow, there are herbs that cultivate better. We're going to go over all of the fundamentals and advantages of each.

Basil

It is a common alternative for hydroponics, as basil is suitable to hang scent and flavor when used fresh. Those characteristics are lacking on dried basil. But having greenhouses and restaurants to use a hydroponics device for basil herbs is not unusual.

There are about 150 different basil varieties in general, although the more common ones are:

- Basil Lemon
- Sweet Basil
- Thai Sweet Basil
- Genovese Basil
- Basil Spicy
- Basil Purple
- Basil Lettuce

By propagating them or planting cuttings that shape their roots in a week, basil can be grown in both ways. It is a warm-temperature herb, so it is safest to maintain the temperature around 70–80 degrees Fahrenheit. The most used medium for developing basil with hydroponics is the Rockwool blocks. While you can use coconut coir, peat moss, vermiculite, and perlite, these can involve sterilization prior to usage.

Pythium is considered a hazard to Basil seeds. What precisely is Pythium? It destroys many herbal crops and spreads disease. Making sure your growing medium surface is not too humid is the best way to get rid of Pythium or other destroying pathogens.

When you get to harvesting the basil, the upper foliage's top 1/3 to 2/3's should be cut. The plant should keep developing that back so that you can reduce it again. Basil will grow up to 2–3 times before removing the plant entirely and starting fresh is suggested.

Only cut the quantity of basil you need; this prevents the stress of having to hold it in good shape. If you select basil, basil's shelf life is just in days, so it might be easier to keep it developing before it is needed.

Chamomile

If you're a major tea lover, you may want to learn that you can cultivate chamomile indoors on your own. Chamomile has numerous great antioxidant properties, which have been proven to reduce the likelihood of diseases such as heart failure and cancer. Often, they help combat depression and bad digestive issues.

Most would use a seed tray that can float to support the chamomile seeds to germinate. You'll want to remove the weaker ones after the seedlings expand to around 2 inches, and there's just one solid seed per cell of the tray. This may take 1 to 2 weeks for the chamomile seed to germinate. Chamomile is recommended to get light for up to 16 hours every day.

Chamomile has full versatility because it applies to pH ranges. It can vary anywhere between 5.6 and 7.5. Ideally, you'll want to reach 6.5 in the center for optimal results to rise. You should be able to yield your chamomile after about eight weeks.

The flowers may be picked by cutting off 3" of the stem and then drying them in a sunny place on a fabric. Through not picking the flowers completely, you will make replanting even easier, which helps them to seed themselves. For storage, stock your chamomile in a sealed jar in a quiet, cool place.

Rosemary

This herb with leaves that look like needles is an evergreen. The herb may flower in green, yellow, purple, or blue. Rosemary can be used as a medicine to a wide variety of problems such as:

- Heartburn

- Digestion problems

- Loss of appetite

- Headache

- Toothache

- Cough

- Low blood pressure

- High blood pressure

- Insect repellent

Compared to others, hydroponically growing rosemary can result much slower. It could take a harvest time of up to 12 weeks and the seed yields are often very small. They also result much more effective to rise hydroponically.

Such plants are susceptible to infections with the bacteria, mites, and powdery mildew. The most suitable for this plant is an NFT hydroponic system, and they can be treated at temperatures varying from 70 degrees Fahrenheit to 85 degrees Fahrenheit max.

Here are some quick tips to hydroponically cultivate the rosemary:

1. Hold the pH from 5.5–7.0.

2. Moisture levels will stay normal.

3. Provide the herb to a minimum of 11 hours of daylight.

4. You can reap 2–3 times every sowing, and that should be achieved during the year.

Oregano

Oregano is a mint, and for many years, they use this herb for medical needs and cooking. The ancient Greeks utilized Oregano for curing gastrointestinal ailments, urinary tract infections, menstrual cramps, skin problems, and dandruff. Several times they have researched Oregano for its antimicrobic action that wards off pathogenic Listeria.

Hydroponic Oregano grows well in pH levels from 6.0 to 9.0, so the level will decline between 6 and 8 for optimum performance. Rockwool cubes are commonly used to sow seeds that can take one to three weeks to germinate. The Fast Rooters, Oasis Root Blocks, or Grodan Stonewool are all other popular medium.

Oregano is a very slow grower, so it could take 8 weeks before the first harvest after transplanting. If you cultivate outside, oregano likes full heat, and as you rise below the lights, the lighting will not be different. T5 tubing are ideal for proper lighting, so they should be about two to four inches from the top of the plant to prevent the leaves from drying or burning.

Cilantro

From seedling up to the harvest of cilantro, it takes about 50 to 55 days when grown in a hydroponic system. This variety of herb needs no trimming and requires pretty much low maintenance. They can be extracted in part or as a whole.

You know what good cilantro is, too, if you're a vegetable lover. Toppings, salsas, garnishes, that's what you call it. Even if some people don't like the taste, why? The cilantro flavor is perceived differently by many people. It is characterized by some as a new and refreshing taste, whereas others consider it to be soap-like. Theoretically, here's a rundown of why this is so.

Temperatures of around 75° Fahrenheit will stay somewhere below 40° Fahrenheit. Nevertheless, with temperatures of around 60, there are higher germination speeds.

Look out for patches of bacterial leaves, accessible to cilantro. Such locations induce elevated moisture levels and susceptibility to so much humidity.

It does require lots of cooling, but it doesn't have to be overwatered. Even if it is proposed, the oscillating air recreates a sturdier natural environment.

Anise

A seldom thought of herb that has a flavor like licorice. It is also often called aniseed. Although Anise can fend off several popular problems such as digestion, nausea, and cramps, certain herbs do aid.

Although the taste of the licorice sort may make it unpopular to others, it is resourceful for bread, cakes, sausages, and cookies to be eaten. Anise seeds are very fragile and difficult to move, so it is better to encourage the seeds to germinate and expand without shifting them in their own containers. You may notice that the seeds will germinate for up to two weeks.

You want the pH level to be holding from 5.5 to 6.5. 6.0 in the center is the best place to rise. The seedlings also profit from having a wavering fan circulating the breeze softly every day for a few hours.

The easiest way to extract Anise is to cut the plant when appropriate and position it in a safe area clear of direct sunlight to dry out. This can put them upside down, too. They are harvested absolutely as early as the heads appear to look gray. Store away from the heat in an airtight jar. Anise usually has a shelf-life of 1 year.

Dill

Dill is an annual growing herb in the family of celery. In Eurasia, it is most commonly perceived as being grown where it is used to spice milk. Dried or fresh dill can be used in recipes. The stems aren't used when using dill. Growing dill is very easy hydroponically and thrives in this sort of increasing climate.

Hydroponic Growing Tips

Put the seedlings on a Rockwool and press them inward. Keep the Rockwool saturated with nutrients and water waiting for the seedlings to propagate. Propagation can take seven to ten days, but it may occur earlier.

You will then grow the Rockwool directly to your hydroponic device after germination. Maintain the pH spectrum from 5.5 to 7.5.

Enable enough space to expand and note that often dill will potentially rise as high as 3 ft.

Harvest only by cutting the green leaves and scraping the stems as ripe brown seeds emerge.

Culinary Applications for Dill

- Soups
- Sauces

- Spreads

- Casseroles

- Pickles

Medical Applications Include

- Abdominal bloat

- Relief and gas

- Cramping

- Headaches

Catnip

You could choose to raise this herb hydroponically if you have a catnip, primarily for their enjoyment and to provide yourself with some pastime. Catnip is not just used for animals, somewhat contrary to conventional myths and the word itself. Catnip has been known since the 1700s for its capacity to ease indigestion and cramps as used in teas.

The following are several suggestions for budding catnip with indoor hydroponics:

- By using leaf-tip cuttings or seeds, you can quickly propagate catnip.

- Give 5 hours of sunshine.

- Use proper irrigation to provide a constant flow of water. Catnip could be susceptible to root rot, so consider preventing an area that is too warm.

- Look out for the development of molds, which may result from so much misting.

- Eliminate all insect infestations like mealybugs, aphids, whitefly, and scale.

- Don't let the cat get close to your machine!

Benefits of Grow Herbs Hydroponically

As usual, when it comes to effectively growing plants, hydroponic systems arise as the top candidate. Herbs can mostly benefit from the capacity of the watering device to provide a continuous supply of oxygen and nutrients. In a hydroponic system, on average, herbs grow between 25 and 50% faster than an outdoor traditional soil system.

CHAPTER 13.

Growing Mediums, Nutrients, Temperature & Lighting

Different Types of Growing Medium for Hydroponics

Medium Originating from Rock or Stone

1. **Perlite**

Perlite is produced from volcanic rocks heated to extreme temperatures and then erupts like popcorn, resulting in a clear, porous medium. It has existed longer than any other hydroponic medium. Perlite has excellent oxygen retention, made of air-puffed glass pellets, and almost as light as air.

The main reason why it is used as a soil and soil-free mixtures substitute is its ability to retain oxygen. Perlite can be used loose forms, in pots, or in slim plastics sleeves, called "growing bags." Plants are usually installed using a drip feed system in perlite grow bags. Perlite grow bags tend to hold three or four long-term plants.

Perlite's biggest disadvantage is its lightweight consistency, making washing away easy. This disadvantage makes perlite an inappropriate medium in hydroponic systems of flood and flush type or those that would be subjected to strong winds and rains if located outside.

2. **Rockwool**

Rockwool is a molten rock derivative. It is also heated to high temperatures, but then spun into thin, insulation-like fibers. Such fibers are then compressed into cubes and slabs for hydroponic growth or sold loose as "flocks." The cubes are widely used for plant propagation, and slabs are used similarly as perlite growing bags. On the Rockwool slab, a plant is put and grown there.

The roots of the seed grow into the slab. Usually, Rockwool slabs hold three or four long-term plants. Rockwool has long been used as an alternative to fiberglass in building insulation and has been a pillar of commercial hydroponics for the past 20 years. It absorbs water readily and has solid drainage properties, which is why it is commonly used as a seed starting medium and a root cutting medium.

3. Lightweight Expanded Clay Aggregate (LECA)

LECA is a very coarse growing medium. Geolite, Grorox, and Hydroton are some of its common trade names. LECA consists of enlarged clay pellets, which can hold water because of their porosity and surface area.

These media are pH neutral and reusable, making them ideally suited for hydroponic systems. Although lava rocks tend to have some of the same characteristics, they should never be used in hydroponic systems because they change the pH and leave behind a thick residue that can damage different types of equipment.

4. Vermiculite

Vermiculite is a mineral that expands due to inter-luminary heat when exposed to high temperatures. It is rarely used alone; it is usually combined with other growth materials, especially Perlite. Vermiculite is a good medium because it allows the retention of water, moisture, and nutrients.

5. Gravels

Gravel is much the same as sand, with differences in particle size only. The particles of gravel are generally 2 to 15 mm in diameter, while the particles of sand are smaller but still gritty. Sand is more likely to hold water than gravel.

Organic Medium

1. Sawdust

Sawdust was commonly used in industrial hydroponics in British Columbia and Canada, primarily due to its quality. Before use, hardwood sawdust should be composted. You should never use some softwood sawdust because they contain highly toxic chemicals. For short-term growth without composting, Pinusradiata sawdust was successful.

2. Coir Fiber (Coconut Fiber)

Coir fiber has been graciously accepted as a hydroponic growing medium of high quality and is available as a thin, granular substance in several propagation cubes, blocks, Rockwool-like slabs. When used as a growing medium, coir fines should be combined with longer fibers, while fines alone are suitable for raising seeds.

Coir has a high capacity for moisture-holding and air-filled porosity and has a long-term structure. It can be used for several years as a growing medium and sterilized between crops. Some coir supplies that may be contaminated with high sodium levels should be taken good care of. To avoid this problem, hydroponic growers should always choose 'sodium-free' horticultural grade coir.

3. Composted Bark

The use of composted bark has become popular as a peat substitute, providing an excellent seed germination medium, as well as hydroponic substrates. In many cases, the bark is preferable to peat if the right grade is chosen.

Nutrient Solution for Your Hydroponic System

Without nutrients, your plants will die. It is that simple. So, your nutrient solution is the key to getting the entire system going. We touched on the simplicity of basic nutrition trumping everything else but let's go into that in more detail. Your solution can usually be broken down into two stages—growth and flower. On top of these, you can find additives to tackle different nutrient deficiencies based on the different plants you may be growing. While the budget may come into it, choosing the most expensive additives isn't a guarantee of good nutrition.

1. **Root Stimulants**

These are essential for hydroponics. Without these, you cannot get cuttings to root. These will improve the size and growth rate of your plant's roots so that they can better take up nutrients. Your plant needs the roots as structural support as well, without strong roots, it can't stand up properly or support fruit. Spindly, sickly plants are not productive because they are diverting nutrients to structure rather than leaves, blooms, or fruit. Root stimulants are also useful if your plants have root rot, as this can help grow new roots before it becomes a problem and the plant loses its means of taking up nutrition. This is an area where price often means performance and is essential for propagating cuttings and in the first stages of your plant's life.

2. **Bloom Maximizers & Vitamins**

These are additives that are high in phosphorus and potassium. These should be added on top of your base nutrient because the plant is using more of these specific elements to produce flowers. They are one of the most expensive additives and can be extremely strong. If they're not diluted properly, there's a very high chance your plant will suffer nutrient burn; however, they're also very effective at doing what they say. If you're harvesting for the flowers or you want extra flowers, start feeding as your plant shows signs of budding for best results and continue until flowering has finished.

You'll also find certain vitamins like B1 that work as a boost to the plant's immune system and prevents disease. It can also strengthen the roots against root rot and help prevent shock during the cloning process. It is essential to strong vegetative growth and helps to produce the plant's essential oils and distribution of phosphorous inside the plant cells. It helps plants at all stages of their life cycle, which is why it is an important additive.

3. **Bacteria & Enzymes**

As part of the plant cycle, the roots need bacteria to be able to absorb certain nutrients. These solutions contain a Mycorrhizae fungus that attaches to the roots and exchanges the plant sugars there for nutrients. Adding this to the solution helps to improve the plant absorbtion as they are the natural bacterial found in soil. You'll want a Mycorrhizae solution specifically designed for hydroponics. These are especially useful when starting a new crop or propagating because the system will be unlikely to have the necessary bacteria for good absorbtion.

You can also find enzyme solutions in the same area. Enzymes are active components in your system that break down some of the larger macronutrients into a smaller molecular form that plants can absorb better. They're also useful for preventing algae and can help plants absorb starches better, which makes for a higher sugar content in the fruit.

4. **Sweetener**

This is only a necessity for fruiting plants and you only need this during the flower and fruit stage. This is an extra fuel boost for your plants and can enhance the flavor. Basically, sugars fuel the microbes in the roots and improve sugar content in the plant itself. These also contain a selection of amino acids which are proteins used to build the fiber of the fruits. It is a mix of complex and simple carbohydrates at the core, but depending on the type, you may also see flavor enhancers that are specific to certain plants.

5. **Flushing**

Before you harvest your plant, you want to clear out the excess solutions and chemicals from it. This means you want to stop using nutrients and solutions about 4–7 days before you plan on harvesting. Flushing agents help remove the bitter chemical taste that can get left behind from heavy metals in the nutrient salts. These build up over time and will ruin the taste of your product if flushing is not done. Flushing agents help clear these out better than water alone and faster. It restores the plants' homeostasis and is essential for food crops. This should only be used in the final stage of growing right before harvesting.

Temperature

If the temperature of the plant exceeds 85 degrees Fahrenheit, the overall growth of the plants will stop quickly. If the gardener is using HID lights, then it becomes challenging to control the temperature. In order to maintain the accurate temperature, the gardener must install centrifugal fans, but in some cases, the fans alone cannot solve the problem.

For this, plan hydroponic gardening when the outside temperature is 55 degrees Fahrenheit or less. Therefore, it is possible to pull fresh air into the garden. On the other hand, you can install air conditioning.

Hydroponics Lighting System

They improve the growth of the plants; you need to have the best growing lights. This must be stated that even if fluorescent lights could give light and replace the natural lights that plants get from the sun, they cannot provide the necessary spectrum that is needed by the plants.

Their high-pressure lights, such as the sodium lights, can produce light that covers the spectrum from red to orange. They also last longer and have a lot of burning energy than the metal halide. They also use reduced energy to perform this function. However, the spectrum of light produced by this light source is quite narrow.

To get the best results, it is advised that you combine the different types of lights to get the results that are close to sunlight such as the spectrum of the sun. You can also cover an ample space with few lights using a light reflector.

Timers

Timers can be used to control lighting, the plants are affected by your lightning and so the timer is of great essence as it helps to remind you when to turn on and off your light; a timer also tells you when to turn on and off your ventilation. It also controls the nutrient flow intervals in your hydroponic garden.

Ballast

This refers to the artificial lighting that is needed in hydroponics. The ballast is a component of systems that regulates the voltage that each individual light bulb receives. Ballasts are usually electronic, digital, or magnetic.

Electronic ballasts do not use wire and steel core, rather they rely on electro components to regulate the voltage received by a bulb. On the other hand, magnetic ballasts use the electromagnetic system to regulate the amount of voltage a light bulb receives. The digital ballast is the most efficient of all, as it integrates the latest computer technology that makes it smaller and better than the others.

CHAPTER 14.

An 8-Step Formula to Raise Your Seeds Successfully

Materials

The first budget-friendly build that we are going to look at is the deep-water culture. This is one of the easiest ways that you can use to get started quickly and easily—if you can mix your nutrient solution, assemble an air pump, and put some plants into the system, you can use this sort of garden with ease! This is a great starting point for beginners because it is not technical—you are simply leaving your plants in net pots, submerged in the garden.

The system will require:

- An opaque tote storage container and lid (commonly found in 18-gallon sizes at any big-box retailer, but any size will work here if it meets the water requirements for your system)

- An air pump and air stone

- Net pots (verify that these are the right size for the full plants that you are going to be growing)

- Growing medium of choice. A common choice is using expanded clay pellets on the bottom of the net pots, with cubes of Rockwool as starters for seedlings placed atop the clay.

- Nutrient solution

- Tools to cut holes in the lid of the storage container

This build is quite simple. Remember, when assembling this, you need to have the plants ready. If you do not, then only assemble the system and wait to fill it with the nutrient solution until your plant starts.

8-Step Instructions

To build this setup, follow these steps:

1. **Gather everything that you will need:** It is always best to have everything all lined up and ready to go before starting. Make sure that the container you will be using to create your reservoir is lightproof, and if it is not, you can treat it with certain light-blocking spray paints on the exterior to try to prevent light from penetrating the nutrient solution. Also ensure that you have all of the tubing that you will need for your pump, and the right size of net pots.

2. **Prepare the growing tray:** In this system, your growing tray is more of a big tray that will suspend the growing pots into the nutrition solution. Measure out the lips of the net pots that you are going to be using and cut just slightly smaller than them. Then, cut out the holes and ensure that they fit. Make sure that your pots are assembled in the proper space as dictated by the plants that you are growing.

3. **Drill a hole for your tubing:** Near the top of the container, you are going to want to drill a small hole, just large enough for the tubing of your air pump. This will allow for the lid to sit firmly on top of the container while still providing a way for your air pump to be looped through.

4. **Add the air stone:** You want your air stone or stones at the bottom of the system. You will want each of these to work thoroughly to ensure that your water is well-mixed and aerated. Feed the tubing for the air pump through the hole you drilled and attach it to the stone with the other end attaching to the pump.

5. **Prepare the nutrient solution:** This is one of the easier steps— all you have to do is follow the instructions for the nutrient solution of your choice. You will simply read the ratios that you will be trying to mix and follow the guidelines to make it happen. Make sure that you place your container where you want it to be, as once you add the solution, it will be heavy and difficult to move. Add the nutrient solution to the container. You will want to fill it up enough so that it submerges the net pots without flooding when you add the pots at a later step.

6. **Prepare the net pots:** Now, you must prepare your net pots. This is quite simple, just fill them up with your growing medium. Then place your plants into the pots as well. The plants will be just fine if you leave them in the starting cubes of Rockwool.

7. **Put it together:** Take the lid to your system and attach it to the reservoir filled up with the nutrient solution. Place each of your net pots into the holes that you have cut. Turn on the air pump.

8. **Allow the system to run:** All that is left is to let the system run. Use lighting if necessary or leave in the sunlight if it is not. Make sure that you check water levels regularly, especially as your plants start to grow and begin to use up more water than they used to. Fill up, as necessary.

Managing Plant Nutrition

Problems fall into three possible classifications:

1. **Nutritional** – There is either too little or too much of one or more specific nutrients.

2. **Environmental** – Conditions for the environment are not ideal.

3. **Pathological** – One or more organisms tamper with the plant's health. Such organisms are called pathogenic agents.

Physiological Problems

There are several environmental factors, which, unless properly controlled, can lead to the damage of a crop. Frost or extreme supply of sunlight may burn fruit or leaves, and fruit may break, and leaves may discolor. Some of the commonest issues are detailed below.

Cracking: Lack of water or excess water may cause a split in the skin of different crops. Occasionally, newly picked carrots split up. Tomatoes that suffer from water shortage and that are exposed to high temperatures may split.

Blossom root rot: A common tomato problem is when the tomato bottom appears to be brown or black and leathery. Typically, it occurs when there is a low supply of calcium combined with erratic growth, causing stress in the plant. This problem is also associated with irregular and variable water supply and varying temperature conditions.

Crooking: This is where the fruit is warped (for example, cucumbers tend to be excessively curved). Crooking has been directly linked to poor temperature, humidity, or nutrition control.

Common Diseases and Their Control in Hydroponics

Alternaria

This blight normally affects leaves and occasionally stems. Symptoms are typically spots and often develop clustered circles as they grow. There are several varieties of Alternaria. Most of them are regulated by Zineb. A spray of copper will regulate some of these.

Anthracnose

Two different groups of anthracnose infections, which can be classified by their symptoms, are:

- Dead spots are a common symptom.

- Symptoms include abnormal growth of some parts of the plant (e.g., an elevated boundary around a depressed central area of undeveloped tissues). Different fungicides can manage anthracnose. Copper sprays control some varieties, others by Zineb and other chemicals.

Botrytis

A gray fuzzy moldy proliferation that develops on roots, branches, fruits, and berries. Botrytis occurs in damp, rainy conditions. It is necessary to remove affected parts and burn them instantly. Preventive measures include increased airflow and decreased moisture. It is possible to use thiram and dichlofluanid fungicides to control these infections.

Downy Mildew

A plant's upper leaf with this disease shows yellow discoloration or dull splotches sprouting underneath with a gray mold. It occurs under most circumstances and is regulated by Zineb.

Fusarium

Symptoms may include yellowing of the leaves, stunted growth, wilting, and dropping of leaves. Commonly, proper sanitation should regulate fusarium.

Phytophthora

There are several modes of Phytophthora ranging from the disease of new seedlings stem to other forms that affect nutrient uptake in very large plants. Symptoms are often drastic and can cause the plant to suddenly die. Remove contaminated sections and clean affected areas. Fongarid will control some modes of phytophthora effectively and reduce the spread of others.

Powdery Mildew

The disease occurs in dry, tropical, humid conditions. A chalky white growth on leaf surfaces is the principal symptom. Sulfur sprays or dust would usually provide regulation.

Water Management

Water Requirements

Plants in their habitat need both water and oxygen. Sometimes, the trick to successfully grow plants is to provide the right delicate balance between those two. Typically, too much air means too little water, and usually, too much water means insufficient air. Throughout aggregate culture, a well-drying medium (e.g., gravel) will typically be combined with a moisture-retaining medium (e.g., vermiculite) to achieve the necessary water retention balance.

Water is composed of 90 percent of the total weight in many fruits; the water content of leaves is 80 percent and that of seeds is 10 percent. In addition to its function in the plant parts, composition water is also essential for the movement of nutrients into the plant and waste products out. In a plant, everything migrates in a dissolved state. If water is not replaced constantly, the cells lose turgidity, and the plant wilts.

Excess Water

Symptoms of Excessive Water

- Development of long, slender seedlings. This usually occurs when the plants become too close together and the soil, as in glasshouses, is warm and humid.

- Presence of growth cracks (in fruits of tomatoes and heads of cabbages or carrots).

- Increased size of cells.

- Lengthy internodes (longer distances between buds and stems).

- Cells bursting (when viewed under a magnifying glass). Typically, this is due to poor irrigation or overwatering. Excess water can cause stunting, diebacks appearing on top of the plant and, in extreme cases, can lead to death. In a wet situation, there is a greater probability of infection with rots, molds, and other fungal diseases.

Symptoms of Water Deficiency

- The first and more common symptom is that the growth rate will gradually start to decline.

- Leaves gradually shrink (although no sign of discoloration).

- Later the branches get shorter, and the flowers and fruits become smaller.

- The plant also draws water from half-grown fruits of some watery fruits (e.g., strawberries, lemons, cherries, etc.) allowing the fruit to wither away.

- Appearances of diebacks from the leading shoots can happen, leading to death in extreme situations.

- A case of water shortage may be due to underwatering, poor root system, excessive drainage, or sometimes intense heat (i.e., water is sometimes dried up from the leaves faster than it can be absorbed by the roots in hot and windy conditions).

Water Relationships

Before constructing an irrigation system, an understanding of the relationship between the root environments, plants, and water is required. The root environment consists either of a solid substance consisting of particles of different sizes and shapes that mesh together imperfectly to form a dynamic system of pores and channels or an enclosed environment filled with water in either a gaseous or liquid state (or both for NFT).

With a solid material, the medium gets saturated as pore spaces are filled with water. This can happen after irrigation or rainfall. A medium will only stay saturated when there is no unrestricted draining of excess water. The amount of water that a medium can hold at saturation is dependent on the volume of available pore space. That is known as the capacity to saturate.

Moisture can be divided into three types within a stable medium:

1. **Gravity water**—This water can only last for a short time in the medium before it flows under gravitational force.

2. **Capillary water**—This is the primary source of water for plant growth, appearing on solid particles as a thin film or as particles in the pore space. The surface tension holds it up in place. (When gravity has drained all the free water, an equilibrium is achieved where the surface tension binds all the remaining water so that gravity is unable to expel it. This condition is called field capacity.)

3. **Hygroscopic water**—This is a thin film of water so firmly held to the solid particles that it cannot be absorbed by the plants. Through a process called transpiration, plants use water. The plant acts as a pump, drawing water (against the forces that hold it in the medium) into the roots of the plant, stems, and leaves from where it is lost through evaporation to the atmosphere.

Evaporation happens as water is drawn into the air and temperature, humidity and wind are determined by climatic characteristics.

If the temperatures and the rate of evaporation are high, a plant will need more water from the medium than when it is low. Plants are ready to use free water; however, there is a need for increased suction to remove surface tension holding water.

When plants reach a stage where they can no longer draw sufficient water to meet their needs, they may start dropping. This is also the wilting point. If at this stage water becomes available, the plant will recover; however, if it continues without water, it will reach a point where it is beyond recuperation.

This is regarded as the persistent point of wilting. The difference between the permanent wilting point and the moisture content of the soil is known as the water available. The amount of water retained, and the amount tightly bound, can vary from medium to medium.

When to Irrigate

The region between the wilting point and the field potential is critical in irrigation, intending to preserve the level of moisture within this zone. It has usually been observed that plants take most of their needs from the upper half of the root zone and thus only about half of the available water is expended.

Therefore, irrigation is generally required when roughly half of the water available is used up. Hence, when the medium is at field capacity, the amount of water to be applied to a crop is half the water available in the root zone of the plant. The timing of irrigation applications depends on how fast the plants use the available moisture and this is usually dependent on climatic conditions and nutrient availability.

Also important is the rate at which water is supplied through irrigation, and it is governed by medium rates of infiltration, i.e., the rate at which water passes into the medium. If it can be absorbed by the medium at a rate lower than the water is supplied, runoff may occur, and water may be wasted. The ideal situation is where the rate of application equals the rate of infiltration.

Plants greatly require water to grow and survive. Nonetheless, the amount of water needed can differ from one plant to another. The two principal factors affecting how much water a plant needs to survive are:

1. **Plant Variety**

Some certain plant types have the ability to retain water for subsequent use within their tissues. This is not possible with other plants.

2. **The setting in which the plant grows**

When there is plenty of water available around the plant, it prefers to remain moister than in open, windy, warm conditions. A plant may suffer from water shortage, but it may also suffer from an unnecessary increase in the supply of water. It is important, when watering a plant, to strike that delicate balance between too little and too much. Overwatering can be as severe as underwatering.

Chapter 15.

Myths about Hydroponics

Hydroponics Is a New Technology

This is a very common myth that is very popular amongst traditionalists. However, as said earlier, it is just a myth. Hydroponic gardening is a very old and ancient field. It is believed that the pharaohs of Egypt loved fruits and vegetables that were grown hydroponically. Even the famous wonder of the Ancient World, The Hanging Gardens of Babylon, were supposed to be hydroponic gardens. In India, plants are grown directly in a coconut husk, hydro at the most grassroots level. It is thus proven that hydroponic gardening is not at all a new technique but an old and ancient science of cultivation.

Hydroponics Is Artificial or Unnatural

Once again, this myth is highly popular amongst traditional thinkers. Such people think that growing plants in water is against nature and is artificial. This is absolute rubbish. The growth of plants is a real and naturally occurring thing and cannot be done artificially. Plants need certain things to grow and thrive and they normally take these things from the soil. In hydroponics, we just replace the soil with water. Plants still can absorb whatever they need from the water and grow well. Unless you consider water unnatural, then you simply cannot consider hydroponic gardening unnatural.

Hydroponic gardening does not involve any kind of genetic mutation or introduction of any unwarranted and mysterious chemicals. This is not a steroid-inducing system but a perfectly natural and safe method of growing crops.

Hydroponics Harms the Environment

This is a ridiculous myth. Hydroponic gardening does not harm the environment at all. In fact, it helps the environment. Water is one of our most precious resources and because of hydroponic gardening around 70 to 90% of water can be saved as compared to the conventional form of gardening. Hydroponic gardening also does not have any fertilizer runoff. This runoff can pollute the soil and rivers, lakes, etc.

Hydroponics Is Very Complicated and Cannot Be Done at Home Unless You Are Exceptionally Talented

Hydroponics is a very easy system of gardening that can be done by almost anyone with a love for plants. An inexpensive hydroponic system can be constructed with simple things such as a bucket, hydroponic growing medium, and hydroponic nutrients. You can definitely use advanced technology and science to create an exceptionally sophisticated hydroponic garden to produce high amounts of yield, but you can also use simple, cheap, yet effective instruments and equipment if you want to do hydroponic gardening just as a hobby. As said earlier, anyone can pick up hydroponic gardening, anyone means people of all ages.

Hydroponics is Far Too Expensive

You can definitely use expensive and advanced technology and science to create an exceptionally sophisticated hydroponic garden to produce high amounts of yield, but you can also use simple, cheap, yet effective instruments and equipment if you want to do hydroponic gardening just as a hobby. You can work on a limited budget and produce excellent and fantastic results with ease if you are dedicated to your garden.

Not Widespread and Limited to Developed Nations

This is a rather bizarre and ridiculous myth. Hydroponic gardening is done in every corner of the world.

People do hydroponic gardening in places where the climate is unsuitable for the growth of plants or in countries where the quality of soil is not suitable for a good yield. It is also commonly used in developed and developing countries, such as the USA, where the soil has been abused and is no longer cultivable. In British Columbia, 90% of all the greenhouse industry is now based upon the hydroponic gardening system.

Hydroponics Must Be Done Indoors

Hydroponics is generally cultivated indoors because people don't have a place to cultivate plants outside but rather to relax. You can easily grow a hydroponic garden outdoors as well. A benefit of constructing a hydroponic garden indoors is the fact that you can control the lights. Outdoors you need to depend on the sun for the light. It is not impossible or hard to do hydroponic gardening outdoors. It is even possible to do soil gardening inside the house if you know how to do it.

Hydroponics Don't Need Pesticides

Well, this myth is very common but unfortunately false. You do need pesticides for a hydroponic garden, but the soil-born pests are eliminated naturally because there is no soil. There are other kinds of pests that you need to protect your plants from. You should ideally only use pesticides when you feel that your plants are under attack. To avoid the attack of pests, keep a close eye on your system. Never enter the dark room when you are unclean or have come from outdoors, especially from a garden or a park.

Hydroponics Produce Huge Plants

This myth is slightly true. Every seed like every other living thing has a genetic code that has all the coding that determines the size, weight, yield, etc., of the plant that the seed will produce. Hydroponics is a well-developed system, but it is not a magical system that can force a seed of cherry tomato to grow a beefsteak tomato plant. But, it can help you to grow the best cherry tomatoes with the seed though.

It is quite hard to grow a seed to its highest point in the soil as the makeup of the soil varies from place to place. Although the components of the soil can be controlled and manipulated, you cannot have 100% control over them. However, in the case of hydroponic gardening, you have total control and freedom on the components. You can easily manipulate them, so as to grow the best plants easily. Hydroponic gardening also consumes a lesser amount of energy as compared to soil gardening. This reserved energy is used by the plants to produce more and more yield. The plants become healthy, their foliage is dense, and their flower and fruits delightful.

Hydroponics is Used Primarily for Illegal Purposes

This myth, unfortunately, has some truth in it. However, like every other thing in this world, you can use hydroponics for a good purpose, as well as a bad purpose. Sugar is a very tasty and sweet product, but if used wrongly, it can give you diabetes. Similarly, dynamite is a very useful product, but if used in an improper way, it can be dangerous. Hydroponic gardening is no different. Often, law enforcement officials talk about hydroponic gardening when talking about marijuana and such illegal substances. Many people thus form a relationship or connection between the two things and start believing that hydroponics is exclusively used to grow illegal substances. Yes, it is true that people do use hydroponic systems for illegal purposes, but people use cars for illegal purposes too. If you cannot stop using cars, you should not stop using hydroponic gardening as an alternative kind of gardening. Remember, any power is good only as long as it is in safe hands. Power itself is not corrupt. The people who use it are corrupt. Likewise, hydroponic gardening is not wrong or illegal. The corrupt people who use it for their illegal benefits are wrong.

CHAPTER 16.

Pest Prevention and Troubleshooting

Common Hydroponic Pests

While there are many pests that can try to make our gardens their home, there are certain pests that show up with more regularity than others. These pests fall into five key categories: spider mites, thrips, fungus gnats, whiteflies, and aphids. If you find yourself with an infestation of pests, it is a safe bet that they'll fall into one of these five categories.

Spider Mites

Out of all five types of pest, spider mites are a particularly annoying one. While they are less than a millimeter long, these little guys are actually tiny spiders. Because they are so small, they have a tendency to start damaging your plants before you even notice that they have taken up in your garden. Spider mite damage will look like tiny brown and yellow spots on the leaves of your plants. While they don't look like anything serious when there are only a couple of bites, this damage accumulates quickly to really wreak havoc on your garden.

To spot a spider mite infestation, there are two key signs to look out for. While the damage to your plants can be a telltale sign, it doesn't specifically tell you that spider mites are the problem. To spot a spider mite infestation, you should check your plants to see if you can spot any spider webbing. Another way to check for spider mites is to use a tissue or clean rag to gently wipe the bottoms of your leaves. If you come away with streaks of blood, this will tell you that you have a spider mite problem.

One way of handling spider mites is to wash your plants down with a hose or powerful spray bottle. The force of the water can often knock the mites off of your plant and drown them in the growing medium. Spider mites also have some natural enemies ranging from ladybugs to lacewings, and you may consider adding these beneficial insects to your garden to feed on the spider mite population.

Aphids

Aphids like to feed on the juices of the plant, and you can find them chewing on stems, leaves, buds, fruits, or roots. They are particularly drawn to the newest parts of the plant. If you find that your leaves are misshapen or yellowing, checking the bottom can reveal aphids. They also leave behind a sticky substance referred to as honeydew. This sweet substance can actually attract other kinds of pests, so aphids are particularly annoying little critters. This substance can also lead to the growth of fungus, like sooty mold, which can cause branches or leaves to turn an unpleasant black color. Aphids are also able to carry viruses from one plant to another, so they can help nasty pathogens to spread quicker.

Like spider mites, spraying water on the leaves can dislodge them and leave them with a hard time finding their way back to your plants. If the infestation is large, dusting your plants with flour can constipate them and help convince them it is time to move on. Wiping down your plants with a mixture of soapy water can also help to kill and drive them off.

Thrips

Like spider mites and aphids, these little guys are also tiny. Often, they are only around 5 millimeters long. It can be hard to spot these little guys, but they leave damage that is clear as day. If you start to see little metallic black specks on your leaves, you probably have some thrips snacking off your garden. Leaves that thrips attack will often turn brown and become super dry because the thrips like to suck out their juices.

Thrips are small and are either black or the color of straw. Because they are so tiny, they look like dark threads to the naked eye. They like to feed in large groups and will fly away if you disturb them. They stick their eggs into flowers and leaves and they only take a couple of days to hatch, so a thrip infestation can seem like it just happened out of nowhere.

Make sure that you inspect your plants for thrip damage and remove any that are infested. Hosing off the plants will also help to reduce their population. Ladybugs, lacewings, and minute pirate bugs all feed on thrips and can be beneficial to your garden.

Fungus Gnats

Fungus gnats are an odd one. Adult fungus gnats have no interest in harming your garden. But their larvae enjoy chewing on the roots of your plants, which slows the growth and opens the plant up for infection. In extreme cases, fungus gnat larvae can actually cause the death of plants. They really like areas with a lot of moisture and high humidity.

Adults typically live for a week and in that time lay up to 300 eggs. It takes half a week for the larvae to emerge but when they do, they start a two-week diet where their main dish is the roots of your plants. When they feed on your plants, they cause them to wilt, stunt their growth, and cause a yellowing of their leaves. These nasty little things can have many generations living off the same plant.

If you suspect a fungus gnat infestation, then you should inspect your plants by carefully turning up the soil around their stems and look for larvae. If you check a plant and it suddenly lets loose a bunch of adult gnats, then you should dispose of that plant. They really like damp soils, so make sure you aren't overwatering your plants. If you have a fungus gnat problem, then letting your potting medium drain longer will help to kill off the larvae and mess up the development of fungus gnat eggs. You can also spray your plants with a combination of peppermint, cinnamon, and sesame oils. This mixture is called flying insect killer and will help to get rid of gnats.

Whiteflies

About the same size as spider mites, whiteflies look like small white moths that take up residence on your plants. They are easier to spot, but because they fly away when you bother them, they can be hard to kill. Like aphids, they enjoy sucking the juices out of your plant and you see their damage as white spots and yellowing of the leaves.

They tend to lay 200–400 eggs in clusters on the underside of the higher leaves. These eggs hatch in about a week and unattractive little nymphs come out that crawl around on your leaves before they grow wings. These crawlers will spread out from the egg and find a place to start chewing on your leaves. They'll stay in that spot for the next week or so before growing into young adults, which will repeat the cycle of movement-feasting.

Ladybugs and lacewings enjoy eating whiteflies and so introducing them to your garden can help to kill off whitefly populations. Hosing off plants with a strong blast of water will help in reducing their numbers as well. There are a bunch of organic pesticides on the market that you can get to deal with whiteflies. These pesticides can also work for the other pests, but pesticides should be a last resort option, one that you are careful with so as not to lead to undue stress on your plants.

Preventing Pests

Let us turn our attention towards how we prevent these pests from getting into our gardens in the first place. Many of these techniques will help us to identify a possible infestation as it is trying to get started and so they offer us early warnings to prepare ourselves to battle pests. If we keep up our preventative measures and keep our eyes peeled for pests, then we can save our plants a lot of damage and ourselves a lot of time by cutting off the problem at the head.

When it comes to pests it is also important to understand that not every pest is the same. This doesn't just mean that whiteflies are different from fungus gnats. What this means is that fungus gnats on the West coast are going to be different than fungus gnats on the East coast. Not every solution for prevention or extermination will work. A certain pesticide may be used to kill gnats in the East, but the ones in the West might have grown an immunity to it.

One of the ways that we prevent pests is to make sure that we limit their ability to enter our garden in the first place. We can do this in a few ways. Insect screens go a long way to keeping out pests. We also want to limit the amount of traffic in and around our setups. If at all possible, our setups will benefit greatly if they can be protected by airlock entrances as these offer the most secure protection against both pests and pathogens. Airlocks can be doubled up to create a space before the garden in which to wipe down dirt and any insects or eggs that are catching a free ride on your clothing.

In order to see if pests are starting to show up in your garden, use sticky traps around your plants. Yellow and blue sticky traps are both useful, as they attract different pests, so you want to make sure to use both kinds for the best results. Place traps near any entrances to your garden, such as doors or ventilation systems. Also, make sure to place one or two near the stems of your plants to catch those pests that prefer snacking on the lower bits, such as aphids or fungus gnats. Get into the habit of checking these traps regularly as they can give you a great idea of what kind of life is calling your garden home.

While traps will help us to get a head start fighting any infections, they aren't a foolproof method when it comes to avoiding pests. Traps should be used together with personal spot checks. This means that you should be checking your plants for pests a couple of times a week. Take a clean cloth and check the bottom of your leaves. Check around the roots for any fungus gnat larvae. You can check the tops of leaves visually. Look for any signs of yellowing or bite marks as described above.

Make sure to remove any weeds that take up root in your garden as these plants are only going to sap your garden's resources and offer a breeding ground for pests. Also remove dead or fallen plant matter, of course. This includes leaves, but also any fruit, buds, or petals that have been dropped.

Finally, before you introduce any new plants to your garden, make sure to quarantine them first so that you can check them for pests. You can use a magnifying glass to get a closer look if you need to. Give the new plants a thorough inspection, making sure to check all parts of the plant and the potting soil before you transfer it over.

By creating a system and a schedule for inspecting your plants, you can prevent an infestation of pests from ruining your garden or causing you a lot of headaches. A vigilant eye will give you the upper hand in both preventing and dealing with any kind of problem you have with pests.

CHAPTER 17.

Starting a Hydroponic Business

You need to consider a few things when starting a hydroponic system:

Considering Space

Some of the hydroponic systems don't require too much space. You can grow an herb garden on a countertop. However, if you want a large system, then you will need a bigger space. For example, NFT is highly effective for long and narrow spaces. You may consider a large ebb and flow method if you have a big chunk of space. Before you begin the system, make sure that you write down the measurements that you have available and do not go over them.

Considering Resources

You need to consider the resources or supplies each of these systems will need. For example, a drip system will not need too many resources. On the other hand, something like NFT runs a pump and needs lighting, and it will need more resources. You should also consider just how many supplies are needed. Do you have a pump? Or you need to buy one? What about tubing? You need to consider everything cost-related. You should also consider your time as a resource. Do you want a system that can be left alone for long periods of time, or do you want one that is perfectly fine being kept for a while?

Considering Cost

Cost is another huge factor to consider. Just how much money do you want to spend on your hydroponic system? Some systems are simple, and you can build them for $10. However, some systems are quite expensive and demanding on resources. If you do not mind the cost, then an expensive system such as NFT is fine.

Considering Expandability

Also, consider just how much you want your system to scale. A wick system could be great for you if you are just getting started, but if you are looking for a system that will grow with you as you continue to learn and as you decided to expand, it may not be right for you. Essentially, you must consider how likely you are to continue to grow with your garden. If this is something that you are not going to expand upon, then some of the most stringent, smaller methods may be just fine. However, if you hope to turn this into something bigger as you get more practice, you will want to look at drip methods, NFTS, and even the ebb and flow.

Considering Reusability

You must also consider just how much reusability you want. How likely are you to reuse the garden after the first or second use? With some of the more expensive and time-consuming methods, you may find that it is not actually worth the money if you are going to use them once. If you are going to grow several harvests or make your hydroponic garden a staple in your home long-term, then an NFT or other more intensive and expensive methods may be just fine. However, if this is just an experiment with kids, then you may want to stick to some of the smaller, cheaper methods.

Conclusion

Hydroponics has a longstanding reputation as a very successful method of growing plants. The idea is that your plants get the nutrients they need from a water solution you add to their soil. Many people have come to rely on hydroponic systems for their green beans, tomatoes, melons, and more.

Indoor hydroponics has little effect on your growth during the season. Design your cultivation around the ease of your fresh food's requirements. We most want an item in winter when high-quality vegetables are not in our local supermarket. The main reason that the herbs are grown separately is because they are very small in shape and would not grow well under vineyards when the light is close to the ceiling as the grape differs. Lettuce also yields higher in a very different combination of nutrients from vineyards. Finally, the lettuce is grown on a very short harvest period of 30 to 40 days, while the vines continue to grow up to six months or longer.

Lettuce can be sown every few days to supply approximately three transplants a week. It brings you salad to pick every day. The number of plants to cultivate depends on your individual demand for fresh salads. Herbs, with the exception of basil, initially grow very slowly. It takes about 3–4 months to develop well. You can harvest them every day when they grow vigorously. For a full year, they will continue to grow.

Basil requires approximately 6 weeks to get well. The plants last up to 3 to 4 months if the basil is kept well tapped from the start. When the basil is 3 to 4 inches tall, pinch the tip of the wax or slice it after the second to the third node with a scissor. This first cut allows plants to branch rather than if it is cut later and keeps the plants from becoming woody. Then cut the tops of every shoot by 3 inches back to the next or lower set of small shoots, which fork between the stick and leaves. Take this way to give you a plant with many branches that will have less woody growth. That's the trick with rising basil that I find. I personally have cultivated basil for up to six months or longer by regularly cutting it (harvesting). If it fails to bloom, it gets old or nervous. Pinch all the buds really early to keep them smaller. Sow typically approximately four plants per cube to create a plant bunch or cluster. These can be transplanted into the rising bed for 6 to 6 inches.

When you most want tomatoes, peppers, and cucumbers in winter, schedule the cultivation accordingly from November to March. Tomatoes will start to harvest fruit no later than mid-August until mid-November. A cropping cycle lasts 7 months until the end of March. Tomatoes need to be planted for about 100 days. Start a second crop by sowing seed at the beginning of March and start harvesting in June.

Greenhouse peppers take approximately one month longer to mature than tomatoes. It is best to start them in July and in March again. You can use bush varieties less mature than greenhouse varieties for a month or so. European cucumbers take 2 months from seeding to the development of the first fruit. If you want to grow all these crops in the same hydroponic system together, begin the cucumbers in September to prepare the cucumbers by November. Thus, the seedlings transplanted to your hydroponic system all start in the same size and grow together. It helps to raise the lights above all plants at the right level. It also prevents the shading of younger plants by older plants. You'll have two crops a year in total. Start your seedlings in a separate system in your own sun, so that the current plant does not interfere with the transition.

You don't need a huge light, but an 8" fluorescent tube will suffice. Invest in a LED grow light and place it six inches from the plants.

A fan—The fan blows air through the plants to create humidity in the air. Make sure that the fan is small enough so that it doesn't blow too hard; otherwise, you will end up killing your plants.

Rubber band—The most important thing is to make sure that you have a rubber band to tighten up your pots on the wall or wherever you want to place them for easy access.

Hydroponic nutrient—The exact amount of nutrients that your plant needs depend on the size of your pot and how much water they are getting from the water reservoir. However, generally speaking, your plant should be consuming half of their total volume of nutrients per week!

If you think that hydroponics is not your cup of tea, then you are underestimating yourself as there is nothing in the world that is impossible. You just have to gain more and more information regards to hydroponics system so that you cannot do a single mistake while doing it.

It is true that there is no single secret or short-cut of doing hydroponic gardening, but you need to boost up your confidence and positive attitude so that it becomes successful.

Through this book, you have learned the whole system of hydroponics in a simple yet effective manner by which you can boost the productivity of the crops by caring like your own child.

The hydroponics system just needs skilled business-minded and devoted individuals who have a keen desire towards hydroponic gardening so that they will get success. It is not essential that doing this experience in agriculture is required, but they are ready to face every challenge regarding to hydroponic system whether it is pests, etc. If you are hard-working, diligent, meticulous, and organized, you will definitely succeed in the hydroponics system.

Appendix: Monitoring Equipment

pH Meter

pH is a measure of how alkaline or how acidic water is. A pH of 7 is neutral. pH levels that range from 1 to 6 are acidic, and levels from 8 to 14 are considered alkaline or basic.

Different plants have their preferences regarding pH levels. To ensure the best possible growth, you need to have a way of testing and then adjusting the pH level of your water.

For example:

- Cabbage likes pH levels of 7.5

- Tomatoes like a pH of 6–6.5

- Sweet potatoes like a pH of 5.2–6

- Peppers like a pH of 5.5–7

- Lettuce and broccoli like a pH of 6–7

A pH meter can be obtained from local hydroponics stores or online. You need to calibrate the sensor with the calibration powder that comes with the meter. A basic pH meter will cost you $10 to $20.

Don't use paper test strips for the water because they are inaccurate. Most of the time, a pH meter is offered in combination with a TDS or EC meter, which we will talk about next.

EC Meter

Electrical conductivity is a measurement of how easily electricity passes through the water, the higher the ion content, the better it is at conducting electricity.

All water has ions in it. When nutrients are added to the water, you are increasing the ion content, effectively increasing the electrical conductivity.

EC or Electrical Conductivity is an integral part of the hydroponics equation. The simplest way of explaining this is as a guide to salts dissolved in water. Its unit is siemens per meter, but in hydroponics, we use milli Siemens per meter.

In short, the higher the number of salts in the water, the higher the conductivity. Water that has no salt (distilled water) will have zero conductivity.

Lettuce likes an EC of 1.2 (or 1.2 milli Siemens), while basil likes an EC of 2.

That is why it is so important to know your EC and what your plants prefer, it will help you to ensure your system is at the right level.

However, electrical conductivity needs are also affected by the weather. When it is hot, the plants evaporate more water. That is why you need to decrease the EC in hot summer months. In colder winter months, you need to increase the EC.

- In warm weather, you need to decrease the EC.

- In cold weather, you need to increase the EC.

An EC meter doesn't tell you the specific amount of which mineral or fertilizer is in the water. If you only use a nutrient solution using the right ratios, you shouldn't worry.

Just because it doesn't monitor individual nutrients doesn't mean it's not useful. Salt levels that are too high will damage your plants.

You generally need to keep them between 0.8 and 1.2 for leafy greens and between 2 and 3.5 for fruiting crops like tomatoes. The source of the water can influence the EC reading. More on this later.

Sometimes, you see the recommended nutrient levels listed as CF. CF is the conductivity factor. This is like EC, used in Europe. If you multiply EC by ten, it will become CF.

For example, lettuce grows best in an EC of 0.8 to 1.2. This is a CF of 8 to 12.

TDS Meter

TDS stands for total dissolved salts. You may hear some hydroponics growers referring to the TDS and not EC. These are both used to determine the strength of your hydroponic solution. If you buy a TDS meter, there will also be an option to switch to EC readings.

It is crucial to understand that TDS is a calculated figure. TDS readings are converted from an EC reading. The problem occurs when you don't know which calculation method was used to produce the TDS; there are several different ones.

In general, EC and CF readings are used in Europe, while TDS is an American measurement. But, regardless of which measurement you choose to use, they are both effectively the same thing: a measure of the nutrient levels in your solution.

The NaCl Conversion Factor

This is effectively measuring salt in the water. The conversion factor for this mineral is your micro siemens figure multiplied by any number between 0.47 and 0.5. You'll find most TDS meters use 0.5. This is the easiest one for you to remember and calculate. Most of the meters sold will use the NaCl conversion factor.

As an example, if you have a reading of 1 EC (1 milli Siemens or 1000 micro-Siemens), you will have a TDS reading of 500 ppm.

Natural Water Conversion Factor

This conversion factor is denoted as the 4-4-2; this quantifies its contents. Forty percent sodium sulfate, forty percent sodium bicarbonate, and twenty percent sodium chloride.

Again, the conversion factor is a range, this time between 0.65 and 0.85. Most TDS meters will use 0.7.

For example, 1 EC (1000 micro-Siemens) will be 700 ppm with a TDS meter that uses natural water conversion.

Potassium Chloride, KCI Conversion Factor

This conversion factor is not a range this time. It is simply a figure of 0.55. Your EC meter reading 1EC or 1000 micro-Siemens will equate to 550 ppm.

These are not all the possible conversion options, but they are the most common. The first, NaCl is the most used today.

Dissolved Oxygen Sensor

Plant roots need oxygen to remain healthy and ensure the plant grows properly. The dissolved oxygen sensor will help you to understand how much oxygen is available in the water and ensure it's enough to keep your plants healthy.

If plants don't get enough oxygen to their roots, they can die. A minimum of 5 ppm is recommended.

A dissolved oxygen meter will be expensive for the hobbyist to buy, especially when you are starting. That is why dissolved oxygen meters are generally not purchased by people who do hydroponics for fun. A good meter can cost you $170 to $500 for a reputable brand.

You do not need to invest in one if you oxygenate the water. Oxygenation of the water can be done by using an air pump with an air stone in the water tank. Depending on the method of growing, you don't need to aerate the water.

The oxygen dissolved in the water would be at its lowest during the summer. The water heats up, and the dissolved oxygen becomes less available. While your plants can do very well in winter, they might lack oxygen during summer.

Made in the USA
Middletown, DE
19 April 2022